Ageless Internet

Internet Basics for Boomers and Seniors

by Terry Lynne Hale

AGELESS INTERNET
Internet Basics
for Boomers and Seniors

This book and cover was formatted and designed by Jean Boles
Email: jean.bolesbooks@gmail.com

Whether you found your
THRILL on BLUEBERRY
HILL

Or Got Your KICKS
ON ROUTE 66

the Information Superhighway
Is TOO COOL TO MISS!

DEDICATION

Many, many, people inspired me to write this book. Two people were instrumental in helping me actually get it written.

This book is dedicated to my sister, Victoria Hale, without whose contributions (some sent in an email as early as March 12, 2003) and ceaseless encouragement, this book would not have been completed. Your insightful suggestions and unique creative expression is reflected on these pages. Thanks, Sis—you're the BEST!

This book is also dedicated to my husband, B. J. Wiest, a man who (sacrificed) many a lonely Sunday afternoon in front of ESPN et al, while I wrote feverishly in the office. A man who supports the many paths I've chosen to walk and whose relentless sense of humor is as welcome today as it was on our first date nearly 29 years ago. Thank you, B. J. for all that you do and for the man you are.

ACKNOWLEDGMENTS

This book was written after researching too great a number of sources to mention here. My sincere thanks to the number of authorities consulted who do not receive individual recognition herein.

Special thanks for editing and other important contributions to Victoria Hale, Debra Stafford, and Jean Boles; for inspiration to Dan Poynter, Peter Bowerman, Wayne Dyer, Louise Hay, the late Earl Nightingale, Jim Rohn, Bob Proctor, Mike Dooley, the late Napolean Hill, Shakti Gawain, Chellie Campbell, Jim Edwards, Joe Vitale, the late Cory Rudl, Brian Tracy, Jack Canfield, Dr. John Demartini, Stephen Pierce, Carolyn Myss, Steven Covey, the late James Allen, the late Kurt Vonnegut, Jr., Sark, the late Ralph Waldo Emerson, many wonderful friends and Soul Sisters Ellie, Lorraine and Melanie, the Hale and Wiest families and many more. Gratitude to David Stanley for the author photographs.

CONTENTS

CONTENTS

CHAPTER ONE: INTRODUCTION

1A.

What is this "Information Superhighway" and why do I want to drive it?

Maybe you're someone who has been overwhelmed by technology and think you will NEVER learn what you need to learn in order to find enjoyment on the Internet...

OR, have you spent time searching for a specific item or subject you were interested in only to get frustrated by the misdirection and unrelated search results?

Do you sometimes find yourself in a "time warp" where, what should have been a quick search for your subject ended up eating away an hour or more of your time? And even then, you didn't find what you were looking for?

Have you tried to learn how to get around on the Internet from well-meaning relatives or friends but have been unsuccessful because they aren't effective teachers or because one or both of you get frustrated & give up?

Have you opened a book on the subject only to be panic-stricken by the technological terms and become annoyed by how complicated understanding the Internet seems to be?

Although this book is written by a Baby Boomer for other Boomers and Seniors (who didn't have access to the Internet until school was two or three decades behind us!) everyone who has struggled to understand the Internet will benefit from AGELESS INTERNET.

It is ageless because the Internet is boundless. Young and old and in-between find they share common ground, enjoy exchanging information, photographs, recipes, music choices and have fun playing games. Once you know how to navigate the Internet you've bridged the gap that used to exist between generations. The Internet levels the playing field, offering sites of (shared) interest to people of all ages.

The term "information superhighway" has been attributed to a 1994 statement by Al Gore who said that it "will allow us to share information, to connect, and to communicate as a global community."

Many believe there isn't an all-inclusive definition of the information superhighway. I want you to know—right now—there are plenty of people with more technical expertise, more conceptual brain power and a much more in depth understanding of the Internet, than I have.

What separates me from them is this: I want to share my knowledge and enthusiasm with all who want to learn but are intimidated by the overly complicated books on the subject. **I AM ABSOLUTELY THRILLED AND GRATEFUL TO BE LIVING IN THIS AGE OF THE INTERNET.** And, with a business background training individuals in customer service, sales and research in a variety of industries, I am well equipped to simplify this huge subject in keeping with the K.I.S.S. (Keep It Simple Silly) approach.

I was born in the middle of the Baby Boom generation. As such, I didn't grow up with computers. We weren't even allowed to use calculators in school!

The times they are 'a changin' all right. My grandmother, Nanna, lived from 1899 to 1970 so she didn't get to experience this unbelievable vehicle for connecting with the world! I have a feeling she would have been as excited as I am at the *wonders* of the World Wide Web.

Baby Boomers and Seniors represent two groups whose knowledge of the Internet is largely self-taught. *Even so, there are many people in both groups who truly know their way around the Net.*

This book is for the others—those who have a modest experience with the Web or none at all. *My love for the Internet is the passion that fuels the writing of this book.*

This book will introduce the Web to those who have found it much too overwhelming or way too complex to explore. It will provide basic guidelines, simplified security, and necessary terminology. It will teach you how to search effectively and provide a number of websites of interest to these groups—to save you precious time.

You will learn about "affiliate marketing"—a terrific way to earn money promoting products and services on the Internet. Know this: **I am an affiliate for some products and services** that I believe in. These are products & services I would tell others about whether I made a dime or not because, as my business name, care2shareNOW suggests, I love sharing information!

But, I am truly grateful for the trust you've placed in me by purchasing this book. Thank you! **So, I am not using affiliate links (hidden or otherwise) to make money off any of the suggestions I make for products or services in**

this book. I want you to know these suggestions are to enhance your life, make your online experience as interesting and exhilarating as it can be— without any other agenda on my part.

Since affiliate marketing is a legitimate, honest stream of income (everyone benefits from having *multiple* streams of income) I will employ it in other projects I take on down the road.

It used to be that to learn about something we had to spend hours in the library researching the subject. Now, in seconds that information and so much more is at your fingertips.

No more arguing with friends over what year a movie came out or who starred in a TV show from the 1970s. Now, in minutes—you can get the answers to these and a zillion other questions limited only by your imagination!

- Are you interested in finding a recipe so you can use the leftovers in your fridge?
- Want to know how to get grease out of a favorite shirt?
- Do you wonder when Halley's Comet will make its next appearance?
- Who sang "Wake Up Little Susie?"
- How many kids did Lucy & Ricky have?
- What sensational murder did Truman Capote's book "In Cold Blood" depict?
- How old is Cher?
- Just where in the heck is Timbuktu?
- What is the currency exchange rate between the United States Dollar (USD) and the Japanese Yen (JPY?)
- If it is 6:00 PM in New York City, what time is it in Melbourne, Australia?
- Which movie won the Academy Award in 1978?
- What is iTunes?
- I forgot to mail an anniversary card! How do I send an e-card today?

- How many pickled peppers did Peter Piper pick?
- What is Santana Abraxis?
- What is the median price of a single family home in Pasadena today?
- How fast did the Beach Boy's Little Deuce Coup go with the top end floored?
- What year did Martin Luther King make his famous "I Have a Dream" speech?
- What actor played Mrs. Robinson in 1967's The Graduate?
- Cornell University is located in which eastern city?
- What is the metric equivalent of 39 inches?

By the time you have finished this book, you will know:

- which **Internet Security** programs will keep you safe
- **terminology** that will ease you into the 21st century
- **how to effectively perform an Internet search**
- how to **maximize the time you invest "online"**
- how to locate **authentic review** sites
- about the ISP (Internet Service Provider) options you have and the difference between them.

AND *SO* MUCH MORE!

1B.

How the Internet Works

Continuing with the KISS approach here, we don't need to know all the details – just the basics. Even so, there is a certain amount of unavoidable Techno-Speak… but we won't get too bogged down in it, OK?

The Internet's origins began with the United States Pentagon's formation of ARPA (Advanced Research Projects Agency) in 1957. Evaluation by this group led to the creation of a computer network *for our military* known as Arpanet—designed to survive a nuclear attack.

Twelve years later, in 1969, an educational tool was added to the Arpanet structure, considered the 4th node. A node is a processing location sometimes referred to as a connection point. By 1997, there were 20 million nodes on the Internet.

In 1989, NSFNet or National Science Foundation Network replaced Arpanet.

The Internet is a global network of computers that "talk" with each other electronically. The Internet is made up of two types of computers: SERVERS (which store pictures, information, and all kinds of data) and CLIENTS which is what our personal computers are. Think of a SERVER as "serving" the information to us when we request it.

While the original intent of the Internet was to maximize production and broad range programming, it also became a significant communications tool for academics to share their research.

Today, the Internet is a communications tool for every-user, sharing multimedia experiences, information and ideas. The Web connects one Internet site to another through hypertext links.

In the early 1990s, the commercial sector's sales and marketing departments discovered the astronomical (mind-blowing) reach the Internet provides. Today, for-profit as well as not-for-profit companies rely on the Internet to interact with their customers or contributors worldwide.

For sticklers out there, know that the Internet is distinct from the World Wide Web. Email and newsgroups are not part of the World Wide Web. But, without the WWW, the Internet wouldn't be useful to most people because of its complex technology.

Hypertext links connect one Internet website to another. They appear as highlighted text (often a different color from the rest) and if you click on the link, you are taken to another page. Sometimes a new window opens up but often you find yourself on a site completely unrelated to what you were looking for to begin with.

AGELESS INTERNET will use the terms interchangeably—along with Information Superhighway, cyberspace, the Web and the Net.

Does anyone rule the Net? No. There is no owner, general administrator or governing agency. Although there are standards for transmitting messages everything is subject to interpretation and may or may not be accurate. There is no censorship.

You can find anything and everything. ***There is as much misinformation as information.*** The Internet is an amazing, spectacular and completely engrossing world that like life, offers those who participate the Good, the Bad *and* the Ugly.

If you wonder how many people use the Internet, **consider that this number changes daily.**

According to the June 30, 2010 **Internet World Stats** (www.internetworldstats.com), the estimated world population in 2010 is 6,845,609,960.

Of this number, 1,966,514,816 people use the Internet. This represents an increase of 444.8% since December 31, 2000 estimates.

In **North America alone,** the estimated 2010 population is 344,157,450.

In June 2010, 266,244,500 people use the Internet for an increase of 146.3% since December 31, 2000. It is estimated that an enormous 77.3% of the population uses the Internet!

So, I think you get the picture that the Internet is hugely popular and offers an unbelievable experience to those who refuse to stand on the cyber sidelines a minute longer!

1C.
What Can I Do On The Internet? - For Fun, For Profit, For Education?

- As you learned from the Introduction to AGELESS INTERNET, you can get answers to all kinds of questions.
- You can send and receive emails.
- You can research gigantic databases from libraries, government, museums, universities, hospitals and more.
- You can do your banking and bill paying on the Internet.
- You can participate at eBay and other online auction sites.
- You can shop online. Nearly every established retail business has a web presence. Additionally, there are hundreds of thousands of online retailers selling everything from flowers to auto parts to fragrances to eco-friendly products. If you can think of it, you will more than likely find an online source for it—legal or not-so-legal.
- You can date online. Really. Online dating is becoming increase-ingly popular for Boomer and Seniors uniting would-be couples across the country and around the world.
- You can make money on the Internet. As mentioned above, there are global businesses that do not have or need a brick and mortar storefront. Not anymore.
- You can begin writing about your life and/or your opinion.

BLOGGING has become a fantastic way to share your point of view and engage others to do the same. Today there are all kinds of blogs on all kinds of subjects. One of the more well-known political blogs is http://www.huffingtonpost.com.

- You can create a blog for free at http://www.blogger.com– have fun! Or make money from it!
- You can upload pictures to social networking sites like Facebook.

You can download pictures to use in creative projects like scrapbooking.

🛣 You can create a website of your own about your life and your interests or create a site about a cause you really believe in.

🛣 You can visit museums you might never get to see otherwise; Look at amazing works of art, scientific discoveries and other spectacular exhibits.

🛣 You can "travel" the world, visiting lands and historical landmarks you may not have a chance to experience. With the Internet, you have 24/7/365 access to explore the globe at your leisure.

The SKY IS THE LIMIT –
Let your imagination soar!

1D.
What is Downloading and What is Uploading?

In simplest terms if you send a file to another person's computer they will have to upload your file (to their computer.) If they send a file to you, you will have to download the file (to your computer.)

An FTP utility is what makes downloading and uploading possible. FTP stands for "file transfer protocol." These days, FTP functionality is built into Internet Explorer and some other browsers. There are also free FTP utilities.

There is much written on computer basics. Everything from choosing a computer to how to use software programs like Microsoft Word and how to do photo editing. I've found some books too complicated to understand so for someone completely new to the subject, I can't suggest they read those books.

A couple of books I do recommend for beginners or those with moderate computing experience include:

Absolute Beginners Guide to Computer Basics (5th Edition)
by Michael Miller   And...

Is This Thing On? A Late Bloomer's Computer Handbook
by Abigail Stokes.
ENJOY!

1E.
How We Navigate (Get Around) The Net

You and I use an **ISP** (Internet Service Provider) which dictates the speed with which we get around on the Net. You may hear terms like high speed and broadband which seem to be used interchangeably. By contrast, the slower, dial-up connection is called narrowband. Now, there is Techno-Speak in this chapter that I'm unable to avoid. You may just want to skim over it & pay attention to the BOLD print listing the ISP choices available.

CABLE is currently the fastest of all connection speeds- about 50 times faster than normal dial-up. This ISP method provides service through the same coax cable as is used for your cable TV service. It requires a modem. It is always on, no waiting and you have full use of your telephone line. The connection speed can be affected by the number of local subscribers online at the same time. Typical speed is 128K per second.

DIAL-UP CONNECTION sends info through telephone lines via a modem. Unless you have more than one phone line, being on the Internet will tie up the use of your phone line. This is typically the cheapest form of ISP at a slow speed of 56K per second. Dial-up often means you have to wait for lengthy dial-up connections in order to get online.

DSL stands for Digital Subscriber Line and like dial-up service, comes through a phone line. However, DSL uses electrical signals humans can't hear. This enables users to access the Internet and use their phone line at the same time. This ISP requires a phone line, a filter and a sending/receiving box that translates data. You must be in the DSL service provider's service area as sensitive transmissions deteriorate over distance.

FIOS means fiber optics high speed Internet.

SATELLITE makes high speed Internet service available in areas that are not serviced by cable or DSL at about 10 times the speed of dial-up. It is always on, no waiting and it doesn't tie up your phone line. This ISP requires a satellite dish and a modem to set up so the start-up costs can be expensive. Check for megabyte limits for downloading and uploading.

WIRELESS is another form of ISP that is always on, no waiting, allows you to use telephone line and Internet simultaneously and does not require a cable line.

For those interested in what others are doing, here are the top ten ISP's, connection type and their respective market shares according to Web Media Brand's ISP Planet Market Research 3Q2008:

- SBC/ATT (DSL, U-Verse, satellite) 15.4%
- Comcast (cable broadband) 15.3%
- Roadrunner (cable broadband) 9.0%
- Verizon (FiOS and DSL) 8.8%
- America Online (US AOL brands) 7.5%
- Earthlink (DSL, dial-up, cable, satellite) 3.0%
- Charter (cable broadband) 2.9%
- Qwest (DSL) 2.8%

- Cablevision (cable broadband) 2.4%
- United Online (counting paid access only) 1.5%

Compare this information to LRG (Leichtman Research Group's) findings that the 19 largest cable and telephone providers in the US acquired 910,000 net additional high speed Internet subscribers in the 3rd quarter of 2009. They state the top cable and telephone companies represent 93% of all subscribers. The breakdown of the top three broadband cable and telephone ISP's with their total number of subscribers—though they may not reflect "solely residential households."

- Comcast Cable: 15,684,000
- Time Warner Cable: 9,167,000
- Cox Cable*: 4,150,000 (*LRG est)
- AT & T: 15,638,000
- Verizon: 9,174,000
- Qwest: 2,951,000

So, presuming this information to be reliable, we're seeing a huge amount of growth in the broadband category of ISP providers, 3Q 2009 vs. 3Q 2008.

Time is money to many of us. But the choice is yours regarding how fast you want to navigate the Net.

CHAPTER TWO: ELECTRONIC MAIL

2A.
ELECTRONIC MAIL: A Fantastic Way of Keeping in Touch With anyone, anywhere, anytime

Email. Seems to me that word has been around all my life, but it certainly hasn't. In fact, I've only known about it since the early 1990s.

According to Darwin Magazine's Prime Movers, January 2002 edition, a computer engineer named Ray Tomlinson is credited with inventing email in 1971. Initially, email could only be sent to other computers using the same network. He wanted to distinguish between messages sent out onto a network and those sent within an office. But, looking at the keyboard with the intent of finding a non-numeric symbol not normally part of a person's name, Tomlinson decided upon the @. Despite giving it just "30 to 40 seconds of thought," the symbol for a place has had sweeping impact on the world of communication. Thank you Ray Tomlinson!

These days if I can't sleep at night, I might just get up and clean out my In-box. While I'm at it I may reply to emails I haven't had time to respond to yet. (Even though sending email in the middle of the night may be discouraged by some Netiquette suggestions, I don't buy into *that*.)

The point is you can reach out to anyone in the world *in a matter of seconds.* Anywhere, anytime, anyplace. How cool is that?!

No stamps, no envelopes, no stationary. (Although you CAN customize your email background with "stationary.") As long as you have an Internet connection or Wireless Internet access, you can send an email from anywhere to anywhere.

Have you forgotten a friend's birthday? Not a problem if your friend is enjoying the 21st century. As long as the person with whom you want to contact uses email, you can send an e-card. Some like Hallmark's Smilebox you pay for while others you can send for free. Be sure to check out the e-card section in the website listing at the end of this book. Read on to learn more about email and the (easy-to-overcome) challenges associated with it.

KEY: (begin with arrows at the top)
Following is a screenshot from my Windows Mail INBOX. (Microsoft Outlook, Mozilla Thunderbird, Apple Inc's and most other "email clients" (as they are sometimes called) will have similar layouts and headings.   Main headings in the Menu Bar are:

File (click on this and you will see options such as New, Save As, Folder, Print, Work Offline (meaning you are not connected to the Internet while working) and Identities, to name some choices. With Microsoft Outlook, for example, you can have separate identities for each email address you use. Many email clients permit 3 to 5 or more different email addresses. This means you can switch

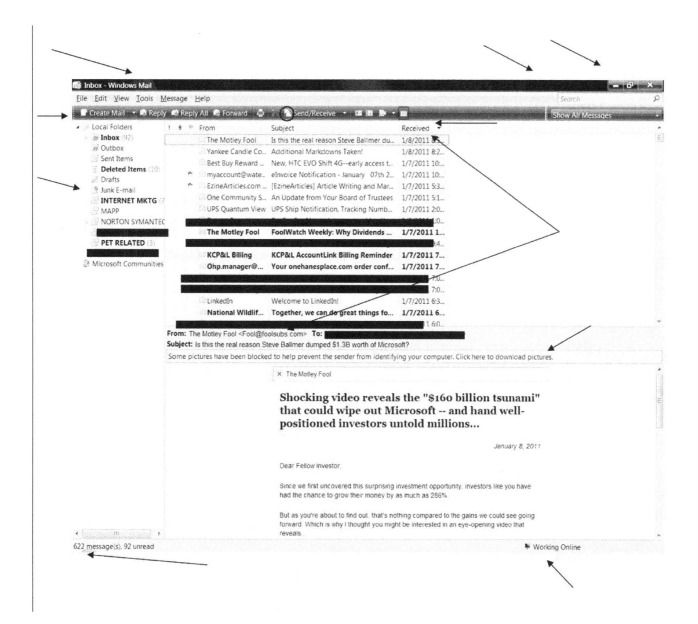

between the different INBOXES to access mail addressed to your various addresses. A family can share a computer and receive their own email using their own "identity." With Windows Mail, all of your email will filter into one INBOX regardless of the number of email addresses you use.

- <u>Edit</u> is an important function. This is where you can select all, copy, move and delete emails. (More on this in another section of Ageless Internet.)

- <u>View</u> allows you to increase or decrease the size of the text, and sort columns among other features.

- <u>Tools</u> is where you can customize your Inbox by choosing options, you can Send & Receive, quickly add the sender of an email to your Contact list, and this is where you can manage Junk Mail options.

- <u>Message</u> is where you can reply to mail, or forward and this is where you can easily manage junk mail by determining if the sender should go into a Safe Sender List or a Block Sender list. This is also where you can FLAG a message to help it stand out. Certain email clients allow you to flag with a *follow up date* and similar options instead of just a flag.

- <u>Help</u> allows you to search an Index of subjects, or access help online at the email clients' main site.

You can use the SEARCH function to try to find a specific email or sender. You can use these buttons to Maximize, Minimize or Close (X) out of this screen. The next section here is a toolbar. By clicking on the various options like:

- <u>CREATE MAIL</u> it will save a little time   (vs. choosing File - New, etc.)

- If you want to <u>REPLY</u> to an email, just click this button and the person who wrote you now appears in the TO box.

- If the email you are reading was sent to multiple email addresses and you want to <u>REPLY</u> <u>ALL</u>, choose this button to do so.

NOTE from the author: use this option with consideration for other people. If you are part of a large group of people who are sent a single email and you want to reply to the sender, keep in mind that not everyone else on the list needs to know (or cares) about your comment.

- Once you have been using email for a while, you will understand why I've devoted a chapter on **MANAGING YOUR INBOX.**

- <u>FORWARD</u> is your choice if you want to forward a picture or file attachment sent to you - to another contact in your address book (contacts.)

- Next you have <u>PRINT</u>, which allows you to quickly print the email.

- <u>X</u> which means to delete the email

- <u>SEND/RECEIVE</u> will let you check to see if you've just received an email that hasn't appeared in your INBOX yet or help expedite the sending of an email. (Sometimes your mail setup is scheduled to send/receive every 30 minutes or some other time frame.)

- Next are icons/pictures for <u>CONTACTS</u>, <u>CALENDAR</u>, <u>FIND</u>, (self explanatory)

- <u>FOLDER</u> which will remove the folder list from your view. Just click it again if you want to see the folder list.

- Finally, at the far right of the screen shot is a DROPDOWN field that gives you the option to <u>SHOW ALL MESSAGES, HIDE READ OR IGNORED MESSAGES</u> <u>AND</u> <u>HIDE READ MESSAGES.</u>

The next arrow is pointing to your INBOX email columns. If you choose to click on <u>!</u> all of the "high priority" emails will be displayed.

If you choose the <u>PAPERCLIP</u> you'll see all of the emails you received that had attachments.

Choose the <u>Flag</u> and you'll see all the emails you *flagged* as important.

Then, you can choose <u>FROM,</u> <u>SUBJECT</u> and <u>RECEIVED</u> to help you locate or sort mail for organizing.

This next arrow is pointing to your <u>LOCAL FOLDERS.</u> This will show INBOX, OUTBOX, SENT ITEMS, DELETED, DRAFTS, JUNK MAIL plus any main folders you created. (A section to come will give you a screen shot of multiple folders I created to manage my INBOX.)

The next arrow shows you that the email being viewed is from The Motley Fool (a fantastic source for investment information. You can sign up for free as well as subscribe for more in-depth investing advice. Sorry, I digress!) It is the highlighted email at the top of my INBOX and you can see on the down arrow the address from which it was sent.

This arrow is pointing out a message from my Internet Security program: I will need to choose to download pictures if I trust this sender. By doing so, the sender may be able to identify my computer. Since I do trust this sender and am not concerned about how they will use any information they may obtain, I will click there to download the pictures. (This is where when you "opt in" to receive emails from a person or a company, it is wise to understand their privacy policy. If in reviewing their policy, I see that my email address will <u>not</u> be used to send to 3rd party companies affiliated with the sender, I'm good. IF, however, they share my information with other companies and I have to take extra steps to opt-out to avoid this, I usually decline to receive emails from them.) It's your choice.

You will see that as of this date, 1/8/11, I have 622 messages in my INBOX, 92 of which are unread. It was just a few days ago that I "managed" my INBOX. So you see, this is proof positive that I've been busy writing this book and have not kept to my personal goal of cleaning up my inbox when it gets to about 250 messages. *It doesn't take long for messages to add up if you enjoy the Internet, subscribe to many sites and have a lot of contacts. (This is another reason for having many folders ..more to come on this.)*

If I wasn't connected to the Internet, this arrow would point out that I was working OFFLINE. Sometimes in order to save money people will chose an ISP (Internet Service Provider) that has a limit to how much time you can spend on line -- in terms of hours. In order to maximize their online experience, they may elect to save web pages in a folder on their hard drive so they can view them later when working offline.

IF YOU DO NOT WANT TO READ AN EMAIL THAT HAS ARRIVED IN YOUR IN-BOX, OR IF YOU DO NOT RECOGNIZE THE SENDER- <u>JUST</u> <u>DELETE</u> <u>IT</u>. DON'T OPEN EMAIL FROM ANYONE YOU DON'T KNOW OR HAVEN'T REQUESTED INFORMATION FROM.

<u>NEVER</u> OPEN AN ATTACHMENT FROM AN   UNKNOWN SENDER —   JUST DELETE THE EMAIL!

2B. *A Look At Windows Mail With Screen Shots*

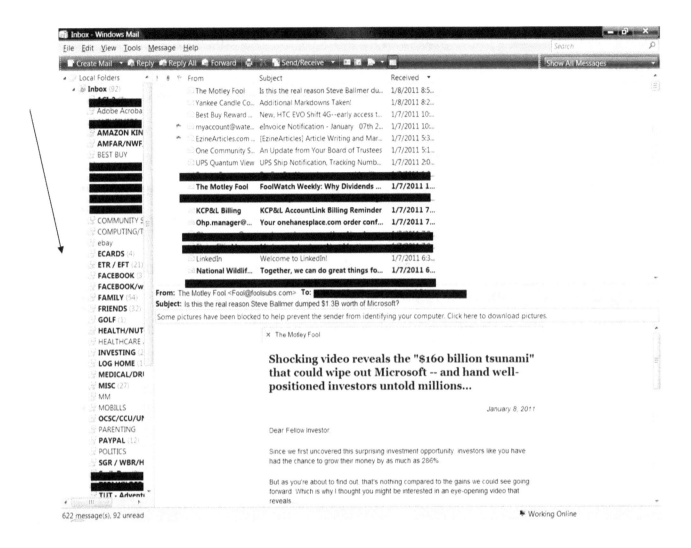

As you can see from this screen shot, I have MANY folders for organizing my email. The number next to the folder is the not the number of emails in the folder but the number of unread emails. This helps you identify things you missed when organizing and you can go through and catch up on those you haven't read yet.

From Family, to Friends, to subjects of interest, and charities you support, it really helps to organize your mail. I often have reason to go back in time, looking for something I read or maybe to print off a travel itinerary of some-one coming to visit who sent their plans to me months before.

Whatever the reason, if it's worth saving, it's worth it to take the time to be able to find it later.

To READ incoming emails in your inbox, click to highlight by name, subject or date received. Notice the highlight/shading on the first email above from The Motley Fool? That is the email whose content appears in the center of the screen.

If you receive an attachment you will see a paperclip off to the left. *If from a trusted source*, <u>double</u> <u>click</u> on the paperclip & the attachment should open. Your ability to open the attachment depends on the type of file it is and if you have a compatible program which permits opening it.

2C.

Setting Up Contacts in Your Address Book & Sending an Email to a Contact

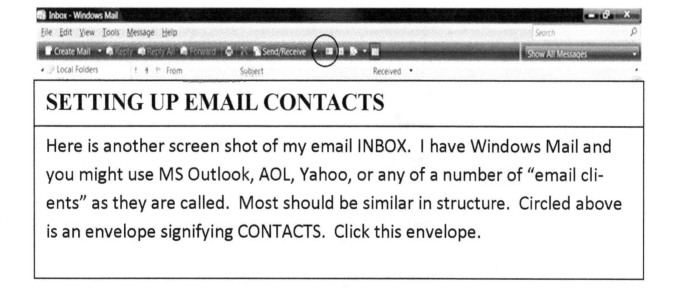

SETTING UP EMAIL CONTACTS

Here is another screen shot of my email INBOX. I have Windows Mail and you might use MS Outlook, AOL, Yahoo, or any of a number of "email clients" as they are called. Most should be similar in structure. Circled above is an envelope signifying CONTACTS. Click this envelope.

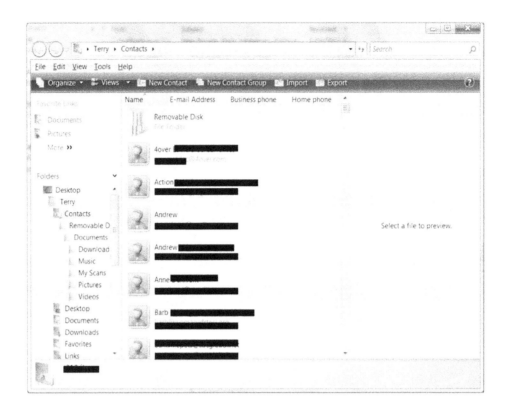

Circled below is NEW CONTACT – click on this button.

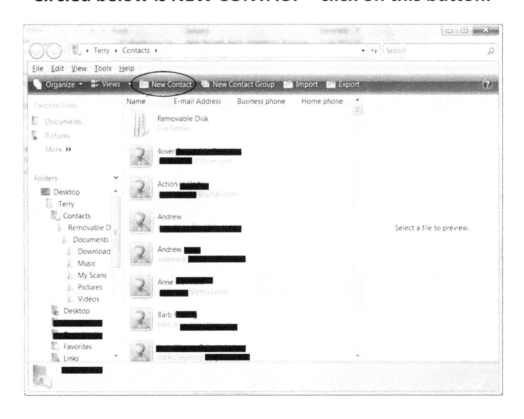

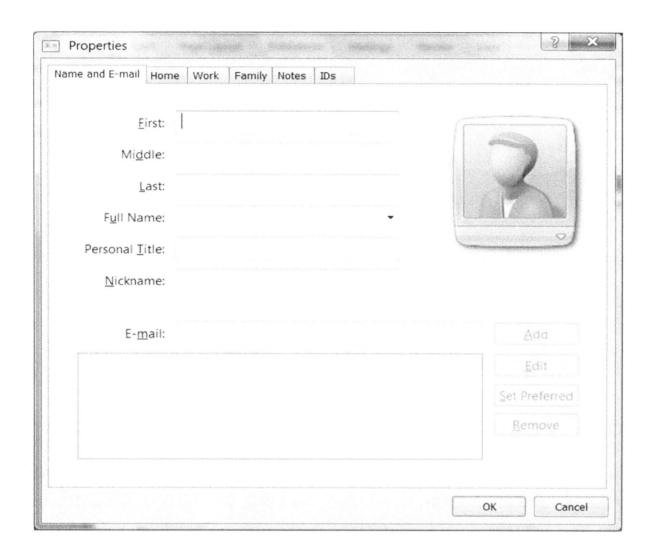

This is a screen shot of the CONTACT PROPERTIES field. Most email clients should have something similar though it may be called an Address Book. It's pretty self-explanatory. You can enter your contact's general information on the first screen and when you add their email address, you can set it as the DEFAULT or preferred address for those folks that have more than one email address. If you like, you can click on the photo above which will let you browse for pictures on your computer of the individual contact you are adding. Select the photo and their picture will be associated with their entry. Your choice.

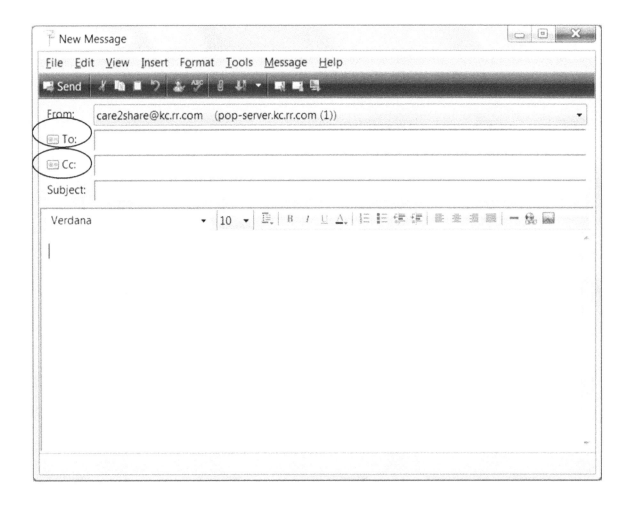

Each tab allows for more information. You can get very detailed like add-ing birthdays and anniversaries. It's entirely up to you how much detail you provide. This is for your use only. Once you've added whatever you desire, click OK and it is saved. Do this repeatedly for every person you want to add to your contact list/address book. When you want to email one of the-se people you will click on CREATE MESSAGE (or New, message, etc.) then click TO and you'll be able to see all the names in your Contacts folder or Address Book. Scroll down to the person you want to email and select their name. The program will default to the preferred email address you associ-ated with that person. If you want to include other people you can select them by clicking on CC (carbon copy) or BCC (blind carbon copy—no one else but you will know they are copied on the email) and select the recipi-ents in the same manner as above. Check out Amazon.com for many books about Email for Beginners for more information. Now, let's send an email to a contact..

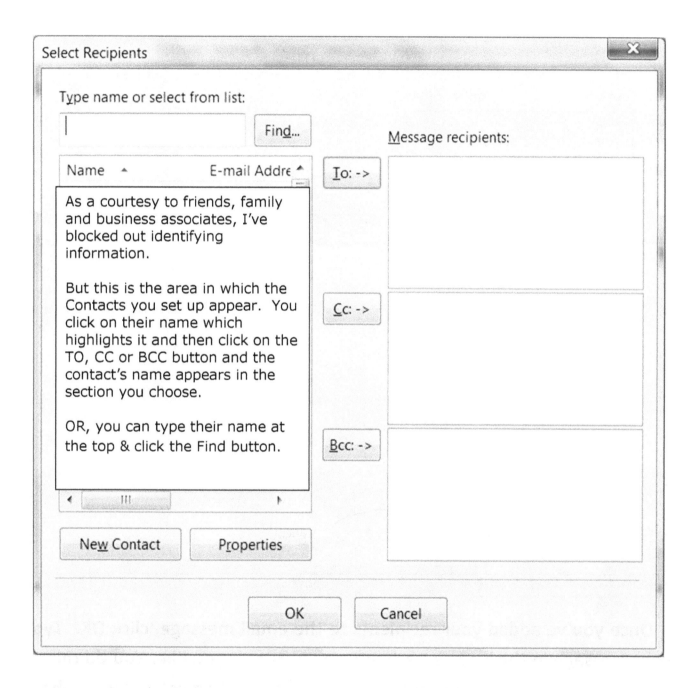

Select Recipients

Type name or select from list:

Find...

Message recipients:

Name ▲	E-mail Addre ▲

To: ->

As a courtesy to friends, family and business associates, I've blocked out identifying information.

But this is the area in which the Contacts you set up appear. You click on their name which highlights it and then click on the TO, CC or BCC button and the contact's name appears in the section you choose.

OR, you can type their name at the top & click the Find button.

Cc: ->

Bcc: ->

New Contact   Properties

OK   Cancel

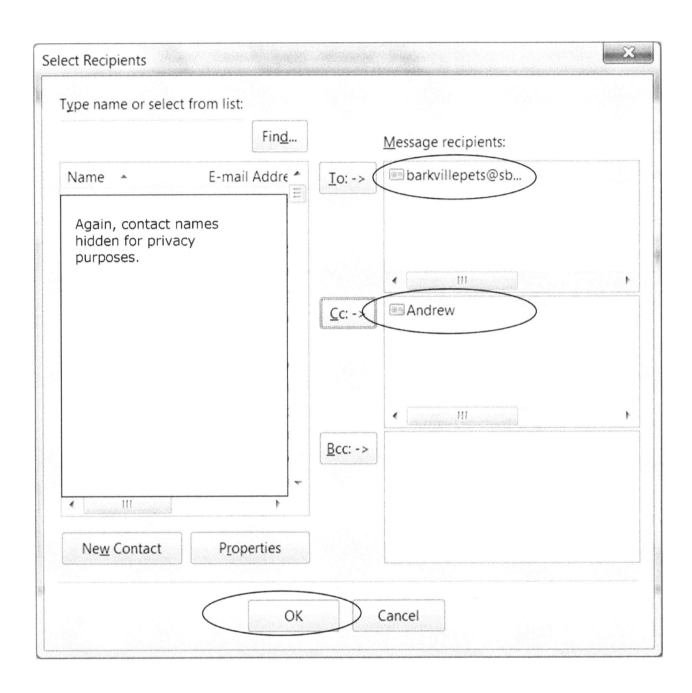

Once you've added your recipients to the email message, click OK. Type your message in the body, attach a file or picture if you like. You do this by clicking the Insert tab, choose file attachment and then select file or photo from your hard drive.

Once you've found it, select it and click OPEN. It will become attached to the email. Then, click SEND and your email is on its way!

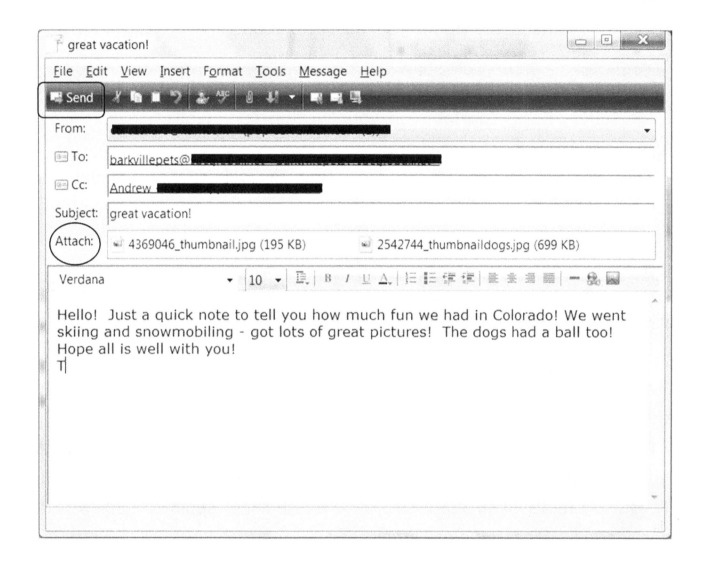

2D.

DETOURS to Productivity

(About Your Email Inbox)

Many people who were excited to get online back in the 90s and begin emailing friends and family quickly became disillusioned with the process.

Unlike letter writing, email correspondence is in "real time." With snail mail (as traditional mail is referred to) a person has time to respond at their convenience, often responding to a letter within a week or two.

The immediacy of email can be demanding. Add this to the "indelicate" tone of email and your lack of a prompt reply can be misunderstood by the sender. Unlike a letter where you use more words to convey emotions or to be more diplomatic, the essence of email is to abbreviate, to write short brief passages. (See "Emoticons" elsewhere in this book.)

Sometimes a quick, terse reply can be misinterpreted. Just as in personal conversation, being courteous in your written communication goes a long way. (See "Netiquette" elsewhere in this book.)

It's up to you to determine how much time you will devote to emailing. Let family and friends know you'll keep up as best you can but to take no offense if you don't respond. *The point is to have fun and enjoy your online experience.*

This writer sent out an email a couple of years ago advising my contacts that I wouldn't be "forwarding" chain letters. Chain letters often include vague threats such as bad luck might come to you if you don't forward. Likewise, there are many that tempt the reader with "good fortune" if they forward to their contacts.

There are all kinds of chain letters including prayer-related ones. These types of letters are often "tracked" giving less than honorable people yours (& your contact's email addresses) for them to send "spam" to. Spam is the number one offender of email inbox chaos.

Here is an excerpt of friendly (and I believe pretty accurate) advice that came into my email inbox recently:

1) Any time you see an email that says "forward this on to '10' (or however many) of your friends", "sign this petition", or "you'll get bad luck" or "you'll get good luck" or "you'll see something funny on your screen after you send it" or whatever—it almost always has an email tracker program attached that tracks the cookies and emails of those folks you forward to.

The host sender is getting a copy each time it gets forwarded and then is able to get lists of 'active' email addresses to use in SPAM emails or sell to other spammers.

Even when you get emails that demand you send the email on if you're not ashamed of God/Jesus --- that is email tracking, and they are playing on our conscience.

These people don't care how they get your email addresses—just as long as they get them. Also, emails that talk about a missing child or a child with an incurable disease "how would you feel if that was your child" —email tracking. Ignore them and don't participate!

2) Almost all emails that ask you to add your name and forward on to others are similar to that mass letter years ago that asked people to send business cards to the little kid in Florida who wanted to break the Guinness Book of Records for the most cards.

All it was, and all any of this type of email is, is a way to get names and 'cookie' tracking information for telemarketers and spammers—to validate active email accounts for their own profitable purposes. You can do your Friends and Family members a GREAT favor by sending this information to them. You will be providing a service to your friends.

And you will be rewarded by not getting thousands of spam emails in the future! Do yourself a favor and STOP adding your name(s) to those types of emails regardless how inviting they might sound! Or make you feel guilty if you don't! It's all about getting email addresses and nothing more.

You may think you are supporting a GREAT cause, but you are NOT! Instead, you will be getting tons of junk mail later and very possibly a virus attached!

Plus, we are helping the spammers get rich!

Hopefully, you've followed the suggestions regarding Internet security so you have email spam blockers employed to screen out many of these unwanted emails.

In addition to email from friends and family, you may receive email from others with whom you've "opted-in." Recent Internet anti-spam regulations dictate that you authorize (opt-in) to receiving email from specific companies. You may want to receive the latest news about your vehicle, your favorite restaurant, CNN, Microsoft and any number of other sources. There are MILLIONS of sites on the World Wide Web.

Most businesses today know their future success depends on having an Internet presence or website. So, nearly every place you visit online has a link for you to accept receiving emails from them. It can be in the form of a newsletter, special offer or a free guide of some kind.

Businesses strive to increase their opt-in lists, because they then have a greater market to target their products & services. So, keep this in mind when you agree (opt-in) to their offers. Many will be legitimate and will provide information of value to you. Later, if you decide you no longer want to receive emails from these senders, reputable firms provide an "unsubscribe" link at the bottom of their emails.

This writer is a big fan of fact-checking before I forward any doom & gloom messages. Basically, I like to check before I forward *anything that claims to be fact.*

Best sources for fact-checking regarding a wide range of topics:

http://www.truthorfiction.com
http://www.factcheck.org
http://www.snopes.com

Here are a couple of other interesting articles regarding email correspondence. I think you'll find them useful.

http://www.truthorfiction.com/virusprotect.htm

http://www.truthorfiction.com/rumors/p/petitions.htm

I've learned a lot over the years and that education has taught me that there is still so much I don't know. I fully expect to hear from folks, that I made some mistakes in the writing of this book. Believe me when I tell you they are *honest* mistakes. *I welcome the opportunity to learn from mine.* Thanks, in advance, for your help.

Please email:
correct@agelessinternet.com

I adore reading and research and am fond of finding famous quotations:

Benjamin Franklin said "Believe none of what you hear and half of what you see."

English lawyer and philosopher, Francis Bacon Sr. said "Read not to contradict and confute, nor to believe and take for granted, but to weigh and consider . . . Histories make men wise."

A Japanese proverb states: If you believe everything you read, better not read.

Love that! ☺

2E.
Managing Your Email Inbox

Whether you use Outlook, Outlook Express or Windows Mail (known as email clients) to name a few, there will be columns in the center of your inbox such as FROM, SUBJECT, RECEIVED. Additionally, there will usually be a counter in the lower left showing you how many messages are in your inbox and how many messages are unread. Please refer to the EMAIL SCREEN SHOTS for help while reading this chapter.

Some ISPs (Internet Service Providers) allow their customers a specified amount of space on their server to host your email. In addition to wanting to keep your INBOX cleaned up for your own peace of mind, you may have to in order to comply with any limits imposed by your ISP. If you exceed the allotted space, email will not be distributed to your inbox.

On the left side of the screen you'll see:

⬡ LOCAL FOLDERS
⬡ INBOX
⬡ OUTBOX
⬡ SENT
⬡ DRAFTS
⬡ JUNK EMAIL and possibly something like Microsoft Communities.

In order to manage your INBOX effectively, you will want to create folders that will be added to those mentioned above.

Keep in mind that many emails can be deleted once you've read them. Every single time you reply to an email, it is recorded in the SENT folder. (You can customize settings to delete, if preferred.)

There will be some messages you definitely want to save. This is why you'll want to create new folders that will appear in the left screen area.

To do this, highlight the email you want to save by single clicking on it.

Then, move your cursor (arrow controlled by your mouse or the laptop touchpad) to: EDIT, MOVE TO FOLDER.

Note: In order to keep your personal folders somewhat alphabetical, make sure that LOCAL FOLDERS is the only one listed here. (You achieve this by clicking on the little arrow to the left of LOCAL Folders- which hides all the other folders.)

Select NEW FOLDER

Type in the name of the new folder, such as "Family." Then click OK. This moves that email to the folder marked FAMILY.

One way to manage your email INBOX is to organize it. For example, let's say you receive email from Hewlett-Packard because you have an HP printer. You may receive weekly emails from HP related to this printer and/or other HP products. You might delete most of these after reading but you may want to save ones specifically related to your printer. Highlight one of these emails. Then, move your cursor to the top column that reads FROM.

 Now, all of your emails will be alphabetized (either ascending or descending) so you can quickly see your entire HP emails.

Highlight, then move to the tab at the top marked EDIT and scroll down to delete for those you don't want to keep. OR, highlight one you want to save, go up to EDIT, choose MOVE TO FOLDER and select the folder you want to move it to.

If you only see "LOCAL FOLDERS" here, click on the arrow to the left to expose your folders. OR, Create a New Folder if necessary.

Likewise, you can do this to quickly save, move or delete a group of emails simultaneously.

Hint: To delete several emails at one time, highlight by single clicking on one of them, and then hold down the CTRL key while you highlight additional emails to delete.

Or, if you have a large number of emails in a row that you want to delete, you can single click highlight the top one, then hold down the SHIFT key and then highlight the last one. All of the emails will be highlighted.

You can then click on the Red X on the toolbar (delete) or choose the EDIT tab at the top & scroll down to: delete. All of the emails will be deleted either way.

Another way to organize your messages is to single click on the RECEIVED column. This organizes your messages by date received in an ascending or descending manner. You can organize by SUBJECT, too.

After cleaning up and organizing your INBOX you may have deleted a large number of messages. If so, single click on the EDIT tab, then scroll down to EMPTY DELETED ITEMS FOLDER.

A pop up will appear asking if you're sure you want to delete these items and if you are sure, click YES. This will clean out the DELETED ITEMS folder.

There may be messages you've SENT that you want to save. You should save them to the folder of choice (or create a new folder) for these. Delete sent messages you don't want to save.

All of the messages in your mailbox take up space. There is so much more to managing your INBOX. You can set parameters, create Message Rules, change the view by sorting.

I won't go into all the details here but there is a HELP tab in every email client that provides a wealth of information. Use it.

2F.
"Netiquette"

When you were a child you were probably told to be polite to others; to say "please" and "thank you" and to be on your "best behavior" in church and in other social settings. You were told to respect your elders and people in positions of authority. Yes, Ma'am or No, Sir were appropriate responses.

This writer could put on a good front, be extremely polite, well-mannered and courteous, but beneath the seemingly good behavior lurked a wild child. Defiant and rebellious, able to astound with 4-letter words a "young lady" should never utter.

Fortunately, I matured. I can still lose my cool, behave unprofessionally, speak unattractively and exhibit poor behavior. But, this happens a lot less frequently now that (what I hated to hear when I was a kid) "wisdom has come with age."

As a lover of words, I've been able to write very effective business letters. I've assisted friends and family with letters of a troubleshooting nature (such as when Company A rips off Individual B) that contain the perfect mix of fact and fiction and a sufficient dose of threat, to obtain the desired result on the underdog's behalf.

Today, my M.O. is to follow the Golden Rule, treating others as I'd like to be treated. Today, I believe that *thoughts become things* and that *like, unto itself, attracts.* These beliefs make for a much more congenial personality. ☺

Though I touch on this subject in the section on EMAIL, it is very important to respect others in Cyberspace. You may already know some basic good behavior like not writing in all CAPS because it means you are shouting and that's rude. Here is a link to "Core Rules of Netiquette" excerpted from the Virginia Shea book, "Netiquette."
http://www.albion.com/netiquette/corerules.html

2G.

Displaying Emotions in Your Email Messages: EMOTICONS

As mentioned before, occasionally email messages are misinterpreted. Unlike the traditional letter, email is an abbreviated form of writing. It is often a few short sentences, swiftly typed and then the "send" button is pushed. The email has no expression, no tone of voice.

Due to the immediate nature of email, it is only after we've hit the send button that we may stop to think, how did that sound? How will the person on the other end take what I've written?

And, again, due to the immediate nature of email, you may find the answer to that question before you've finished typing it. The receiver may have seen your email, possibly misunderstood the tone of it and shot off a quick, terse reply.

When this kind of sequence turns ugly, it is known as a "flaming" and when others get in on the negative action, it is called a "flame war." A flame war is basically an online argument initiated by any number of things including an email, a forum posting or an instant message. Individuals who enjoy causing trouble this way are called "flamers." Many online forums or other message groups ban this kind of activity.

So, several years ago the idea was formed to include "text based" keyboard emotions (emoticons) into an email message so the reader would get a clearer picture of the writer's intent. As far as the origin of emoticons, I won't get into whether it was a Professor at Carnegie Mellon in 1982 or an Aunt writing her niece a letter in 1967…you can research it! ☺

Today, as evidenced by the smiley face above, I entered a text based emoticon and it was converted into a smiley face by the software program I'm using. There are many Smileys in existence today- often included at the bottom of an email & many are free downloads. Smileys are quite animated and occasionally annoying.

Check out Text Based Emoticons at: http://www.sharpened.net/emoticons

Check out Smileys at: http://www.smileycentral.com

CHAPTER THREE:

PREPARING FOR THE JOURNEY

3A.
A Look at Computers

have a lot of respect for Consumer Reports—you can say I am a fan. They provide an UNBIASED view of the products they rate so those ratings carry a good deal of weight with me. Without advertising revenue supporting them, results seen are *presumably* from impartial analysis.

But, I also like to refer to some review sites, like TopTenREVIEWS (a TechMedia property) which does accept advertising. So, information shared in this chapter will utilize both resources.

PC – personal desktop computer

If you want to use a PC you need to decide:

- What programs do you want to be able to run?
- What components are needed to successfully run these programs

🛣 What is your budget for your PC?

From running a household to running a home-based business, certain software programs are essential. Microsoft Word, Excel, Quicken, TurboTax, Internet Security and others are important programs to be able to run. With the growing popularity of digital cameras and camcorders, photo editing and editing of home movies combined with Internet content like streaming videos, it's a smart choice to choose an "entry level" computer with at least 1 GB of RAM (memory) and at least 160GB of hard drive space. IF you intend to become a big gamer (playing lots of video games online) throw this "entry level" discussion out the window. You'll want more RAM, more hard disk space and a really fast processor to play.

But, back to the majority of Ageless Internet's readers:

🛣 Your *processor* (trade names include Intel Pentium, Intel Core, AMD Phenom, AMD Athlon, etc.) affects the speed with which you can run productivity programs without negatively impacting performance.

🛣 Memory allows you to quickly access regularly used information or programs.

🛣 Most PCs have integrated Video/Audio suitable for home use.

🛣 Peripherals like a mouse, keyboard, monitor, and speakers are often included in a PC package.

🛣 The value for the price is an important consideration. Price will be determined by the software, peripherals and other components included.

🛣 Top-of-the-line manufacturers stand behind their products with high quality help via email, phone and online chat. There will usually be a warranty period of 1 to 3 years included in the purchase price.

Using the resources mentioned above, both show appreciation and a good rating for the Dell Studio XPS 8100. Desktop computer prices range from

$310 to $1800 and you should be able to buy a very good PC for around $1000. (There are units called All-In-Ones that include speakers and other components or peripherals that run much higher.)

PLEASE explore your choices to determine which PC is right for you.

Laptop/Notebook

Fun to have for work or play, they're small, and extremely portable. With built in wi-fi (as long as you have Internet access) you can check your email, read the NY Times, and edit that article you're writing, or update your Facebook page. BEWARE that some of these laptops are smaller and lighter weight because they do not include CD or DVD drives- *necessary for running some programs.* The plus side of this is extended battery life.

Important considerations include:

- Size and it *does* matter here. The big benefit to using a laptop is that you have a powerful <u>portable</u> unit. Keep this in mind unless you want to include computing in your daily exercise regimen.
- Battery life. Look for a laptop that holds a charge for several hours. The whole point of this type of computer is that you don't want to have to be plugged in.
- The size of your screen. I once chose a laptop with an 18" screen because I wanted to enjoy better graphics but the weight of that puppy was a killer! Bad move. You can choose a 13" or 14" screen that weighs half of what an 18" weighs! Then again, there are lightweight big screens that come with a super hefty price tag, so it's your call.

The Dell Inspiron 14 looks like a pretty decent choice in a laptop. Laptop prices (largely based on screen size) run from $380 to $2300 and you should be able to get a very good one in the $900.00 range.

Netbooks or Mini Notebooks

Smaller screen and keyboard, these units are less powerful than a laptop although battery life is usually better. They don't have the processing speed necessary for gaming. A 10.1 inch screen is the norm and they weigh half of what an average laptop weighs. Price averages $280 to $430.00.

Both TopTenReviews and Consumer Reports give thumbs up to Asus Eee PC 1015PE.

It is interesting to note that Consumer Reports best ratings for this type of computer starts at 63 (out of 100.)

3B.

TOLLWAYS: Computer Peripherals Like
Printers, Copiers, Scanners

A computer peripheral is a device (typically) plugged into your computer. Peripherals include in no particular order:

- Printers
- Scanners
- Keyboards
- Mice
- Web cams
- Monitors
- Speakers

Do you need these? YES! At least most of them. If you choose to use a laptop instead of a desktop PC, you won't need a monitor, keyboard or speakers since these are part of a laptop computer. Today, many laptops include a web cam built into them.

Your choice of PRINTER should be based on what you intend to print. If price is a major concern when choosing a printer, take into account processing time (pages per minute—PPM—for Black and White—B&W—or color), the cost of replacement ink cartridges, or toner, or imaging drum—as all of these impact the long term cost-effectiveness of your choice.

Printer Types:

Inkjet uses droplets of ink from cartridges (1 to 4) that use cyan, (blue/green) yellow, magenta and black and there are specialty inkjet cartridges some people choose for printing photos. Inkjet printers have come a long way in quality. They print black and white considerably faster than color.

Laser forms images by transferring powdered ink (toner) onto the page passing over an electrically charged drum. (Imaging drum.) They work kind of like plain paper copiers. Laser provides sharp black & white text but they are not known for great photo printing. Color laser printers are much slower than B&W and they're usually fairly large units.

All-In-Ones (aka Multi-Function) offer printing, scanning, copying (and sometimes) fax capabilities. This is my personal favorite for desktop publishing because they are also space saving. I've used both inkjet and laser all-in-ones for the convenience they provide. Performance-wise, they are comparable to plain printers.

Specialty Photo or Snapshot Printers are compact and produce very good quality 4" x 6" or 5" x 7" pictures-check to see size options on any you consider. These usually print directly from your camera's memory card without needing to be connected to your computer.

Mobile Printers are also called "personal printers" because they're designed for people on the go. Compact, they normally fit right into a briefcase and often have a battery in addition to an external power cord. Memory card readers make it possible to print without a computer.

Copiers became a suspect commercial office machine last year when it was discovered that used copiers (and all-in-ones) could be a privacy threat. An April 2010 CBS report and a September 2010 Consumer Reports Magazine article tells of digital files (of copies, scans, faxes, prints) that are kept on the internal hard drive of the copier.

When discarded or trashed, this information could be retrieved by identity thieves. One example listed is a construction company's discarded machine that had pay stubs with names, addresses and social security numbers. Or another, a health insurer's used copier held data relating to prescriptions and a cancer diagnosis. The FTC is contacting copier manufacturers to make sure they are aware of risks.

More expensive copiers are on the market that automatically erase the last file scanned though they are not widely used at present—presumably because they are higher priced.

These may be valid security concerns for all of our reproducing equipment (home and corporate office) so it's something to be aware of.

Today, most home office copying is done using All-In-Ones. You can still buy Xerox, Minolta, Toshiba, Ricoh and many more if your particular needs warrant high volume copying.

Scanners are another piece of equipment found on all-in-ones but you can still find flatbed and sheet fed scanners. (I'm excluding fingerprint and other off-subject scanners) Scanners are still the machine of choice for transferring photo slides to a computer, and archiving all paper receipts and legal documents. A scanner that works beautifully with paper docs may not be suitable for photographs so; perform your due diligence to find the right scanner for your purposes.

Keyboards are now part of the conversation when discussing mobile phones—in addition to your home PC. But we'll focus on desktop computing here.

Some of the big names include Logitech, Adesso, Microsoft, Unitek, Saitek and Cherry. They are corded and cordless and you can even get (as I did) an illuminated keyboard which really comes in handy during the occasional bout of insomnia. You can buy them with a mouse and without. You can buy them wired or wireless. The options are many. From shape, to weight, to price (ranging from under $10 to several hundred) to with receiver (for home theater PC use) or without. The way the keys feel when you type, and the ergonomics of the keyboard make this a pretty subjective decision when it's time to replace or purchase your keyboard.

Mice are another category of peripheral for which choices abound. You can spend under $10 to a few hundred dollars. Believe it or not, there are even mice that cost over $1000 but I'm NOT going there.

Some big names in mice include Microsoft, Sony, Logitech, HP, Adesso and ACCO. Wired or wireless, mini or full size, finger rests or without – you have a lot to consider. The appearance of mice varies considerably from the early days of computing! You can choose by movement technology, color, and orientation to name a few choices.

Another peripheral with lots of choices include the **WEB CAM** or **WEBCAM.** This device typically hooks onto your monitor or comes with its own stand so you can make videos or visit family and friends in "real time." This is called video chatting and can be accomplished with popular programs like:

- Yahoo Messenger   http://messenger.yahoo.com/
- Skype   http://www.skype.com
- Google Chat   http://www.google.com/chat/video

You can buy webcams for under $10 to several hundred and yes, there are some over $1000.00. HP, Ezonics, Logitech, and Micro Innovations are some of the brand names. They come in different colors and shapes but image quality should be your main concern when evaluating a webcam. I'm not a *video chatter-box* but am pleased with one I bought for $50.00. Most laptops bought today come with webcams.

Monitor is the part of the computer that displays what you're looking for- it is the TV screen of your computer. In fact, today people sometimes buy a monitor instead of a TV – especially if they are looking for cost-savings. A monitor is useless without a computer, or receiver or a cable channel providing programming.

The quality of the display, the viewing angle and ease of operation are all part of what you should evaluate in considering a PC monitor. Most monitors are flat screen models and pricing will vary based on the size of the screen – today this is typically 19-20" on the smaller scale and 22" – 26" on the larger. Some brand names include Dell, Apple, LG, Acer, ViewSonic, Gateway, HP and Sony. You can spend over $100 to several hundred on a good quality monitor.

Your choice of **Speakers** should be related to what you intend to use your computer for. Watching videos or playing games requires a different speaker than that of what a user who doesn't play games or watch many videos would require. You can pay as little as under $10 for PC speakers.

However, for a good quality PC speaker system for listening to audio instruction, occasional YouTube videos, MP3 or iPod music, listening to a TV show or movie now and then, plan on spending from $75 to $400.00. This range gives you a lot of good options. Some brand names are Logitech, Altec Lansing, Sony, JBL, Klipsch, Creative Labs, Bose, and Harmon/Kardon.

You can spend a lot more than $400 but if you have an average "ear" like many of us, you don't need to. (I have a brother-in-law who is a musician and he has a musician's ear. He can walk in a room & tell you if the treble is off or bass too low. Now, *he* may want to spend more on his speakers! ☺)

3C.

Leaving The Bogeyman/Boogeyman Out Of The Trip

Right here, right now, accept that if you want to enjoy your online experience you MUST have an Internet security program. What's more, you MUST keep it UPDATED regularly.

If you choose to go with a subscription based security program (my choice) it is something you must renew every year.

Some of the scary stories you've heard or read about regarding Identity Theft, viruses, Trojan Horses, Worms and others are completely true. Many are not. Elsewhere in this book, you'll find out where to go to verify if a story is accurate or not.

Keep in mind, everyone who uses the Internet should be protecting their own security and in so doing, protects their friends' and families' security, too. Many well-meaning people have sent jokes (often attachments) to others and unknowingly transmitted a virus to them.

There are many security options available. From *stand-alone* security products like anti-virus, anti-spam, and spyware to security *suites* (*my* personal preference) that have multiple products built into them. Some stand-alone products are available as free downloads – some you pay for.

Consider that with most free programs, support is limited to FAQ's and tutorials whereas products you pay for often come with toll free support—for a limited time you can contact a live person, etc.

Security Suites, having many products built in, are more expensive. I find them to be more user-friendly and to offer a very broad range of security features.

Today, many web browsers include their own valuable protection. These browsers also offer updates – sometimes called "security patches" which you should download promptly in order to maximize safety. You see, as security is breached, software manufacturers learn how to undo or otherwise resolve the breach to keep their users safer.

As promised from the beginning, Ageless Internet is a *simplified* guide. Many books are written on the subject of Internet security if you want more detailed information.

For our purposes here, I'm going to steer you toward Security Suites, because of their ease of use. When and if you choose to become a more advanced computer user, you may prefer to customize stand-alone products to create your ideal security scenario.

Here are some basic security guidelines you should always follow:

- Don't download games, music or any software from unfamiliar sites. (They may carry malicious software intended to infect your computer.)
- Don't click on hyperlinks in email messages that direct you to provide any personal account numbers or other passwords, etc. (This is a common ploy of cyber thieves.)
- Don't open attachments (signified with a paper clip image) that come with email messages unless you know the person or company that sent it and are expecting it. (Beware of friends and family members who mean well but do not practice safe computing themselves.)
- Use common sense on social networking sites by controlling private data you exchange.
- Back up important data on a regular basis.
- When your security program offers updates, use them! Regularly.
- Update application software at the publishers' site to avoid viruses.

Your computer's operating system is another consideration when it comes to security, safety and vulnerability. According to Consumer Reports June 2009, "Apple computers were much less likely than PCs to have been attacked by viruses and spyware, but Macs can transmit infected files to PCs..."

So, it is important that you select security software appropriate to your operating system. Also pay attention to the "System Requirements" on security (and any software) you consider for your computer.

You have to make sure you have sufficient memory in your computer (more of an issue with older computers) or security programs can really slow you down. Subscription **Security Suites** demand greater resources than stand-alone products because they're providing multiple security programs with one convenient download.

A good security suite will provide anti-virus, anti-spam, and anti-spyware components; it will have firewalls in place and provide regular scans of your computer files. You should set your program to perform automatic security updates, to scan incoming and outgoing email, etc.

There may be privacy settings, child safety restrictions, etc. One subscription will normally license (cover) 3 computers or users. These programs have so much more detail than I'm covering here so please utilize the manufacturer's site if you have questions about how to set your preferences.

Again, please understand you are *subscribing* to a security program or suite (of programs) so your subscription must be renewed annually. THIS IS CRITICAL to you being smart and safe online!

According to Neil J. Rubenking, PC Magazine's (www.pcmag.com) Lead Analyst, The Best Security Suites for 2010 (article dated 02.25.10) the evaluation included:

- Panda
- McAfee
- Norton

- eScan
- K7
- BitDefender
- F-Security
- Trend Micro
- FortiClient
- CA
- Zone Alarm

The Editor's Choice Awards went to Norton Internet Security 2010 and 2011 as well as Norton 360 3.0. (This writer is a fan of Norton products, having tried at least two other manufacturers' over the years without satisfaction.)

The review adds that in addition to the Editor's Choices, "you won't go wrong choosing McAfee, ZoneAlarm, or BitDefender" full security suites.

http://www.pcmag.com/category2/0,2806,4829,00.asp

There are free security programs for those folks on an extremely tight budget. Check out PC Magazine's ratings to see their suggestion for free programs in the FIND SECURITY section on the LH side of the screen by PRICE, and choose "Under $100" category.

The most important thing you should take away from this chapter is that safety is **CRITICAL** to your enjoyment of the Internet. It's the ONLY way to Keep The Bogeyman/Boogeyman out of the trip!

For kicks and grins, check out:

http://www.monstropedia.org to read about the Bogeyman or Boogeyman and other monster-types that have haunted us.

It's interesting to note that nearly every culture has their version of this urban legend.

3D.

ROAD BLOCKS: Cookies, Phishing, Trojan horse, Viruses, and Worms

To be clear: Thieves on the Internet are making a living. They steal from unsuspecting people vs. the street mugger, whom you know has crossed your path. There are people who sell information stolen from you through various Road Blocks like what you'll read about below. There really is a Black Market for cyber thieves just as there is for offline crime.

You won't have to be as concerned as some about these Road Blocks because you will have invested in an excellent Internet Security program to protect you, as suggested by Ageless Internet.

The definition of a **web cookie** (or browser cookie) is that it is a very small text file placed on your hard drive by a web page server. Since it is uniquely yours, it is like an ID. Intended to track your movements, it provides the server who placed it the ability to see where you go, where you've been. Of course, if you don't provide you name and other identifying information, they only know your cookie code.

When it comes to cookies, there is an upside. Cookies enable us to save "favorites" and help save us time when we return to websites on a frequent basis. Like, registering your purchase of a TV, the cookie that site left on your hard drive enables them to bring up your unique ID the next time you visit. It can save you time.

Websites are happy to place cookies on your server because they gain valuable insight into what interests you, what sites you visit, and much more. But consider how many websites you visit and if each one is dropping a little text file on your hard drive, over time, those things slow you down. Your system can get sluggish.

We actually have some control over cookies. You can set your browser to prohibit any cookies from being placed on your hard drive and you can set it to ask you each time a web server wants to leave a cookie. Or, choose a setting somewhere in between. The process varies depending on the browser you use but is similar.

- In Internet Explorer (or whatever browser you use, like Firefox Mozilla, Apple's Safari to name a few) choose TOOLS
- Then, INTERNET OPTIONS
- Then, PRIVACY (or SECURITY) tab
- Then, select the setting that suits your purpose.

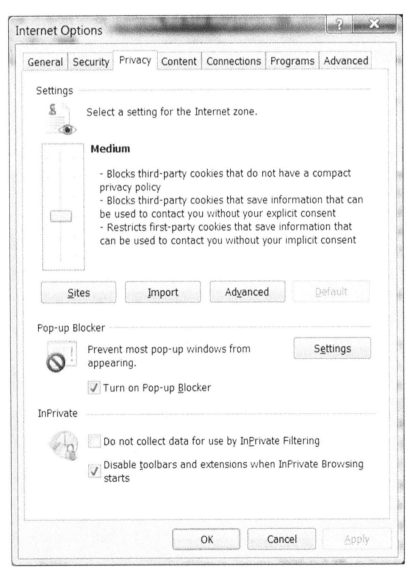

This screen shot is an example from Internet Explorer 8. (IE8) Every browser will have some similar options for restricting cookies. If you select "high" this may prohibit you from effectively saving a website as a FAVORITE. A virus cannot be delivered via a cookie.

Are you wondering which browser version you are running?

With Microsoft (MS) Internet Explorer, if you are running IE7 or IE8, to determine which version you have, go to START menu (lower left) click on the IE icon and then press ALT + H, then click "About Internet Explorer." You will see what version you are running. Check with your browsers main website for help with their particular program.

According to TopTenReviews, the top 5 browsers in 2011 are:

- Firefox (Mozilla) (www.mozilla.com)
- Google Chrome (www.google.com/chrome/)
- Internet Explorer (www.microsoft.com)
- Opera (www.opera.com)
- Safari (www.apple.com/safari/)

Phishing is a particularly nasty practice that technologically savvy con artists use to try to steal identity and consume financial property. They do this by trying to trick people into believing they are at an authentic site, like their bank, for instance and they encourage people, by threatening risk of account cancellation, to enter their account number. Then they can swoop in and clean you out.

This is often accomplished via an email from what looks like your bank or credit union or payment processor always with a threat of some kind that encourages an urgent response on your part. Fight back! PayPal, for example, asks their customers to notify them of phishing attempts by forwarding the "spoof email." (I've always thought of "spoof" as too kind a word for what these thieves are doing...)

As I stress in the chapter on Effective Searching, **ALWAYS** look at the address bar to make sure <u>you are where you think you are</u>. These cyber thieves are getting craftier by the minute and you need to be on guard so you don't fall victim to their scams. The fake sites they create are EXTREMELY close to the real deal and this is how so many people fall prey to their fraud.

Financial institutions like banks, credit unions, PayPal, etc. are ***secure.*** There will often be a green highlight in the address bar when you arrive at a financial institution that shows a symbol of a lock and/or maybe it will read "identified by VeriSign" or something like this.

The bottom line, be on guard. *I don't want to frighten you from enjoying online banking or purchasing—I love being able to use the Net for these purposes!* I just want you to outsmart the cyber criminals. Anytime you are able to "bust" them by sending their bogus attempts on to the authorities (bank, PayPal, etc.) please do so. Over time, these people will slip up & honest people need to stick together and do what they can to bring them down.

Trojan horse is virus software often "dropped" from a website. It may appear to be a helpful program (prior to installing it) but through malicious code it can wreak havoc with your computer, causing pop-ups to come up all over; it can freeze the computer, steal information, or install a toolbar you might not notice. When working in conjunction with a hacker, a Trojan horse can allow remote access to your computer where personal files can be modified or deleted, data stolen, third party malware installed, and any number of other activities detrimental to you. (See Worm below for some of the common symptoms.)

A computer **Virus** is a small software program that, much like the flu viruses we catch and spread to one another, spreads from one computer to the next causing them to function improperly. Most commonly spread by instant messaging or email, this is the reason you are told not to open attachments from any unknown source. Unfortunately viruses may be masked in jokes, cartoons, greeting cards and other seemingly harmless downloads. They might be in audios or videos you download. They can completely corrupt your files or delete your hard drive. They are wicked. Typical symptoms of a virus *may* include:

- your computer runs very slow- much slower than normal
- computer crashes and restarts frequently
- computer freezes or locks up
- you see unusual error messages
- you see a double extension on an attachment recently opened (.jpg.jpg)
- your Anti-Virus program isn't running or cannot be installed
- items don't print correctly
- new icons appear on your desktop that you don't recognize
- programs disappear from your computer although you didn't delete them
- Strange music or other unusual sounds are coming from your speakers

A computer **Worm** is also a virus and is found in email messages and downloaded files. One symptom is that it duplicates itself, tying up your hard disk space. It can infect a file and send a copy of the infected file to all of the addresses in your email contact list. It can install hidden programs such as pirated software which it may distribute and sell. Another red flag is having your contacts report they received email from you with attachments you didn't send. These may have file extensions like .exe, .vbs, .scr. or .bat.

As in life on the streets, crime has found cyberspace to be a profitable setting. WE have to use precaution on the Internet *like everywhere else*. There is no reason to blow these fears out of proportion. Be smart, stay safe.

CHAPTER FOUR: HITTING THE ROAD

4A.

ROADMAP: PLAN YOUR ROUTE
How To Search The Net – Effectively!

I f you have felt frustrated by trying to search for a particular topic because your search results gave you lots of unrelated information, you are not alone. My guess is that many people have become disgusted about using the Internet because of this.

We locate information and find specific websites of interest by using a **"search engine."** Nearly everyone has heard the name "Google" even if they didn't know what it was. Google is maybe the best known of the global search engines. Just like with websites, there is no central registry of search engines. No one has to get authorization to create a search engine any more than they need to get the go-ahead to create a website.

According to Boutell.com (relating to Tom Boutell, a WWW pioneer in Philadelphia) there are "hundreds of language—and country-specific search engines" and tens of thousands that are site specific. AOL (America OnLine) appears to be a search engine but it is actually *fueled by Google* so it would not be considered an independent search engine. When I started writing this section, I could swear Time Warner Cable Roadrunner's SEARCH function was powered **by ASK but today, a week later, it reads "Enhanced by Google."** Very *fluid* information.

While data on the Net is constantly changing, as of this writing it is probably safe to say that of truly independent search engines, the leaders are Google, Yahoo, MSN, Ask and My Web.

(One of them could buy another tomorrow and this would be out of date—not that I have any insight into this- just making a point!)

Some other search engines gaining in popularity include: Duck Duck Go, Yippy, Webopedia, The Internet Archive, Mahalo and Cuil (pronounced "cool.")

My goal here is to help you make the most of your searches – to cut through the B.S. of "sponsored sites" and paid advertising and, yes, even affiliate links that take you to products or services being promoted by others. There are options to increase where data shows up in the search engines and this is called "search rankings." As you can understand, having a site show up near the top or on the first page of a search engine's results increases the chance that whoever is searching will visit that site.

If a search yields 10 pages of results, will you look at results on page 7 or will you limit your actions to the first page or two? Exactly.

What do I mean by the terms sponsored, paid ads and affiliate links?

A "sponsored" site is one whose placement at the top (or side page) of search engines has been **paid for**. The opposite of this are search results that are "organic." To avoid   Techno-Speak we won't get into how search engines work. Just think of organic like you do organic food: without additives or preservatives. You may have seen or heard the term SEO (Search Engine Optimization.) A well- written website, taking into account what search engines look for, means the site has been optimized for search engines. Truly great organic websites practice SEO.

🛣 "Paid advertising" is when a company or person uses Pay-Per-Click (PPC) or Adwords (or some similar method) to increase their **position** in the search engine rankings. I am no expert in PPC or Adwords though I promise you that in order to promote this book I'm going to expand my knowledge on the subject!

🛣 "Affiliate links" brings us to a very interesting subject you need to know about. It has pluses and minuses. Affiliate marketing has made it possible for tens of thousands of people (or more) to leave their 9 to 5 j.o.b.s. (Sometimes referred to as JustOverBroke...) and create a nice income on the Web. By promoting other people's products and services, they receive a commission.

In truth, *I'm hoping people sign up to become affiliates of **Ageless Internet**!* If making extra money by recommending products and services you like sounds attractive to you, sign up to be an AI Affiliate and earn money by recommending this book to your friends and family. And thanks for helping spread the word about Ageless Internet!

It is an amazing process when recommendations help fuel the success of a book, a resume writing service, a widget or a membership site. "Word of Mouth" advertising has ALWAYS been the *premium* method of increasing sales since the beginning of time. Affiliate marketing is the Internet version of this but with a payoff for the party making the recommendation.

Since making money is at the core of Affiliate Marketing, people promoting products have created mini-websites that *appear* to be authentic review sites. Sometimes this trips us up in our quest to find completely honest and accurate information on a product or service.

However, if I want a truly non-biased opinion, I consult Consumer Reports. As mentioned before, Consumer Reports doesn't accept paid advertising so the result of their testing is completely impartial.

http://www.consumerreports.org/

Likewise, if I want to learn un-biased facts about nutrition I may consult the Center for Science in the Public Interest (CSPINET) publishers of Nutrition Action Healthletter, found at: http://www.cspinet.org/nah/

Note: Elsewhere in this book I write about looking at the address bar to make sure you are on the web site you want to be on. Occasionally, the web address WILL NOT spell out **exactly** what you were looking for. This one, for Nutrition Action Healthletter is a good example.

OK, back to Search Engines. Keep in mind a search engine is not a person. It is a program that tries to match your word(s) with pages on the web. Here are some basics:

- To search, enter a word or several words to describe what you're looking for
- Fewer words are better because every word matters
- Keep it simple
- Punctuation is typically ignored
- You can use upper or lower case letters - search engines are case-insensitive
- Be as descriptive as possible

For our purposes here, we're going to review search results from three search engines: Google, Ask and Bing. This is going to fill a lot of pages because I want the screen shots large enough so you can read them. If you're like me, your bifocals (or for some folks, trifocals) have to work overtime reading some web pages! Feel free to skim over this section if you're already an ace at searching the Net, OK?

In the first example, I've entered the search term: **leftover recipes** in Google's search box...**GOOGLE'S first page results for this phrase shows there are 1,280,000 results (also called "hits") and they like to show how quickly these results were found: 0.16 seconds. This page lists four results under Ads on the right-hand side of the page.**

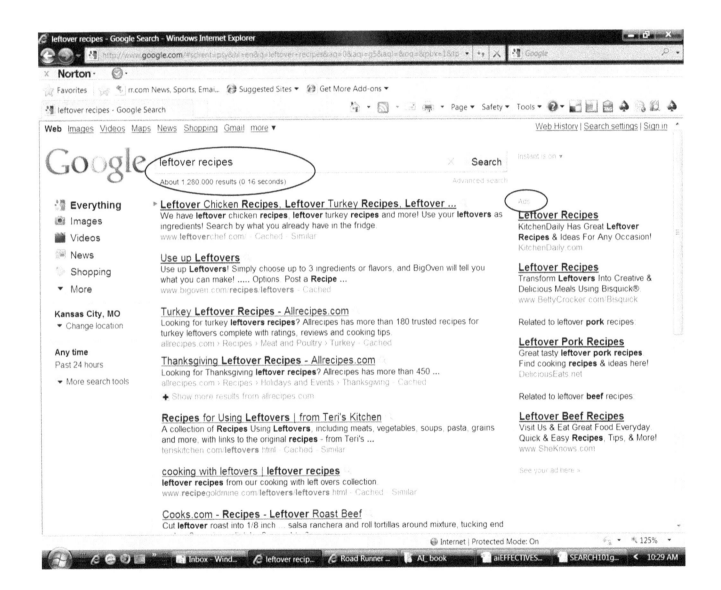

This is the bottom of the previous page; here they list 10 pages (under Goooogle, near the bottom), but with over one million "hits," there will be many, many   pages in all. They also show SEARCHES RELATED to leftover recipes for more search options.

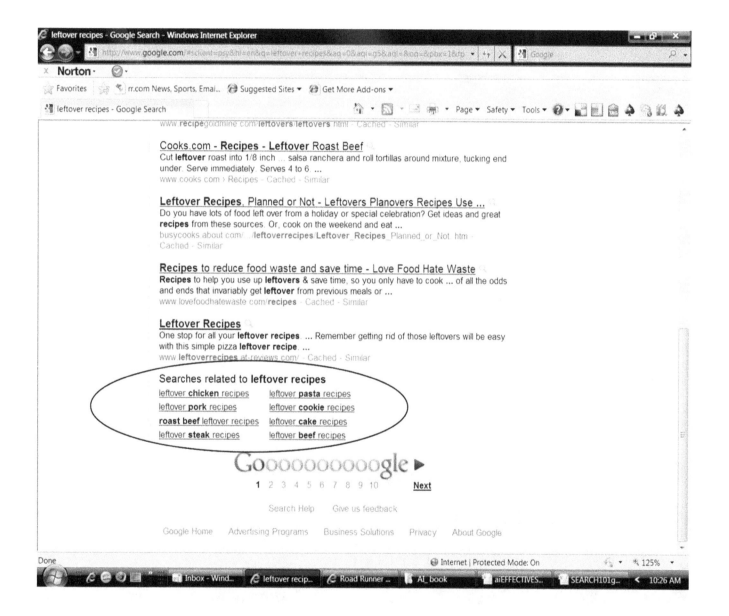

Page 5 (searched and printed just minutes after the first search) and you will see it reads 1,390,000 results (in 12 seconds!) Do you see how fluid information on the Internet is? For all we know, 100,000 new websites were added in that space of time!

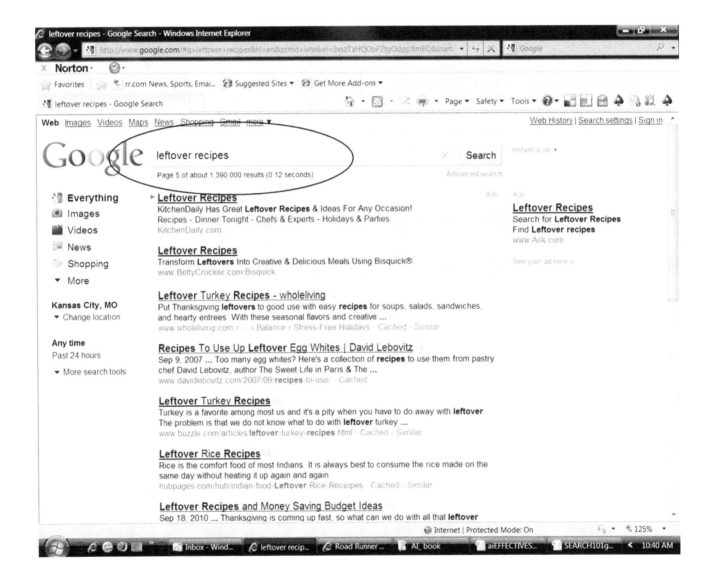

Using the same search words, here's what the first page of search engine ASK.com reflects. ASK'S first page shows a listing from *leftoverchef.com* followed by five Sponsored Results. ASK shows related searches on the right, along with questions related to the search and a history of other terms you've searched for recently.

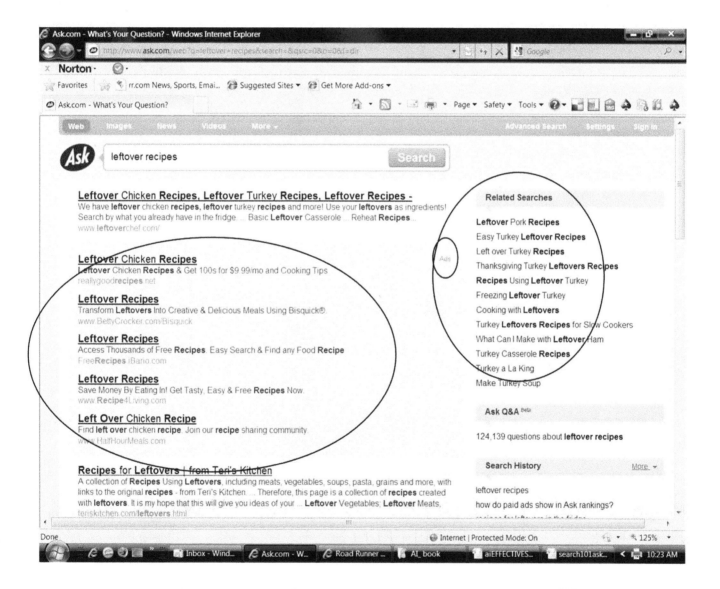

ASK doesn't give a count for the number of results, but the bottom of the first page shows _at least_ 10 pages of results—very likely hundreds more. Notice that their ads show up at the top and bottom of each page- maximum exposure for those folks willing to pay for placement in the search engine. See Page 5 of ASK search results next. You'll see the sponsored sites show up on this page too.

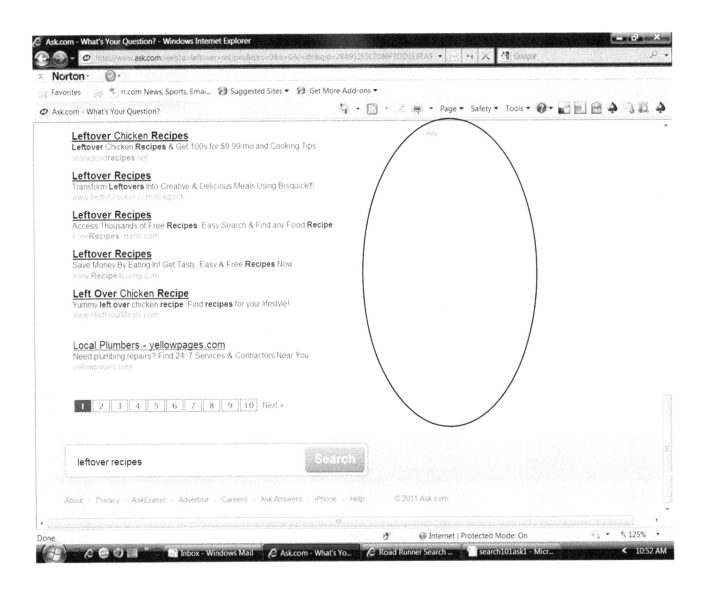

My efforts here are to get you to see certain aspects of the search results page. I'm not partial to any one search engine – I use all of them and in fact, I sometimes use http://www.metacrawler.com

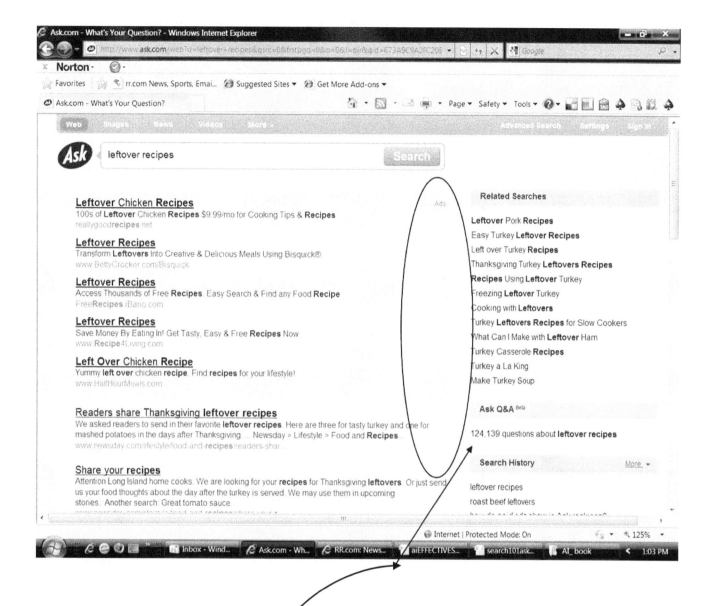

A meta-crawler, sometimes referred to as a meta-search engine, sorts through the results of multiple search engines to provide a more a pertinent group of links. In effect, it searches the search engine *as this one claims. (But, if you notice, ASK has a section called Q & A, and these are questions people ask about leftover recipes. If you're looking for something to do... ☺)*

Now, let's take a look at the search engine BING using the same words, leftover recipes: BING'S first page shows 2,790,000 results. They show one Sponsored site at the top (shaded area) and four more on the right side of the page.

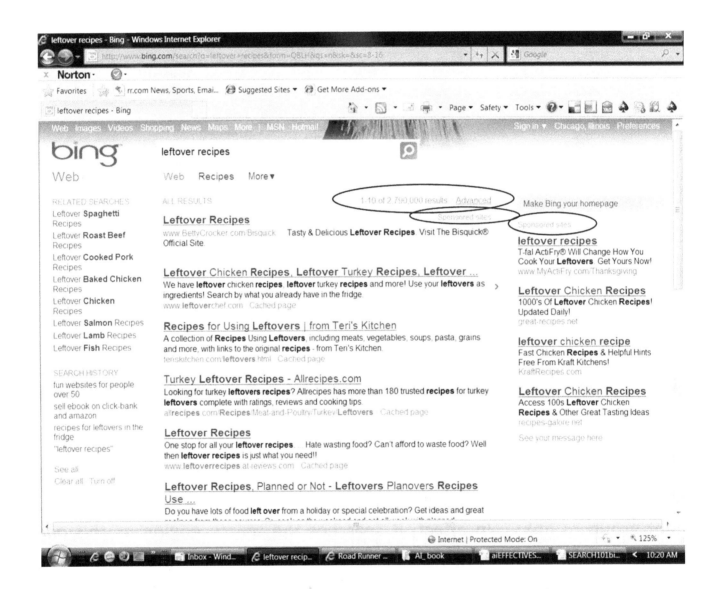

The bottom of the page lists 5 pages + "next" for moving through the results. Note BettyCrocker.com's <u>sponsored site</u> shows up at the bottom <u>and</u> top of the pages. Ads and sponsored sites are *often* located in a colored-shaded box in an attempt to highlight or segregate them. Keep in mind that advertising venues can affect the positioning of a search result even when it isn't stated or in a section called Ads or Sponsored.

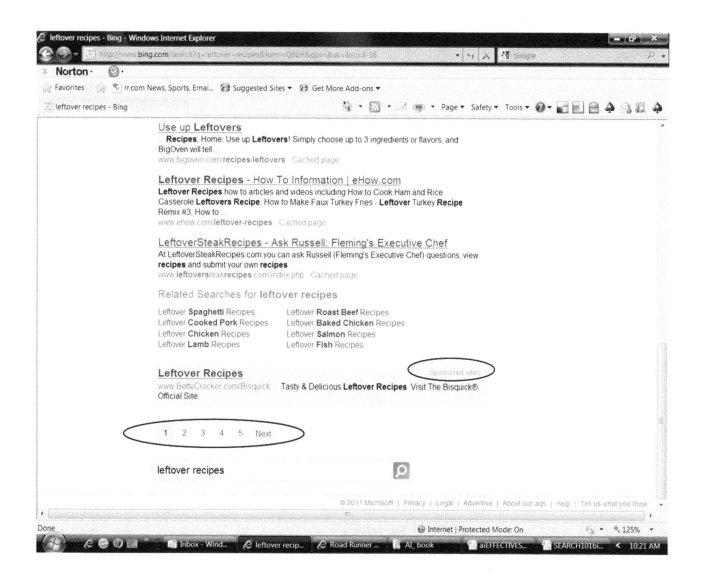

Now, let's be even more precise in our search. Say you bought a very large beef rump roast and have leftover meat you don't want to waste. Let's look at a search for: <u>roast</u> <u>beef</u> <u>leftovers</u> – showing Google first:

Now that we are zeroing in on what we really want, leftover recipes for roast beef, we end up with (only) 223,000 results on the first page of Google.

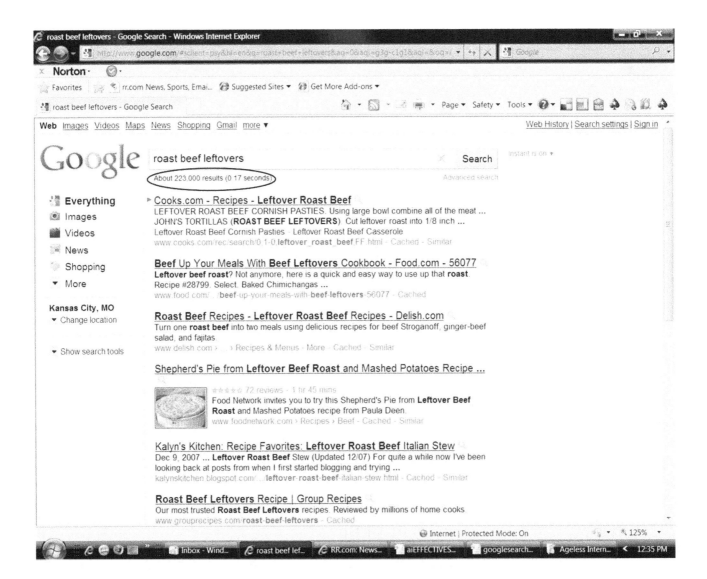

This is the bottom of the first page results:

Following, let's look at Page 5 of this search – see how the number of "hits" has increased to 231,000 in only a few minutes. The Internet is constantly changing!

This Google search result doesn't appear to showcase any sponsored links, sites or Ads.   It may be that Cooks.com's website has excellent SEO (if you recall, this means search engine optimization) so that it is placing high in the rankings – *organically*.

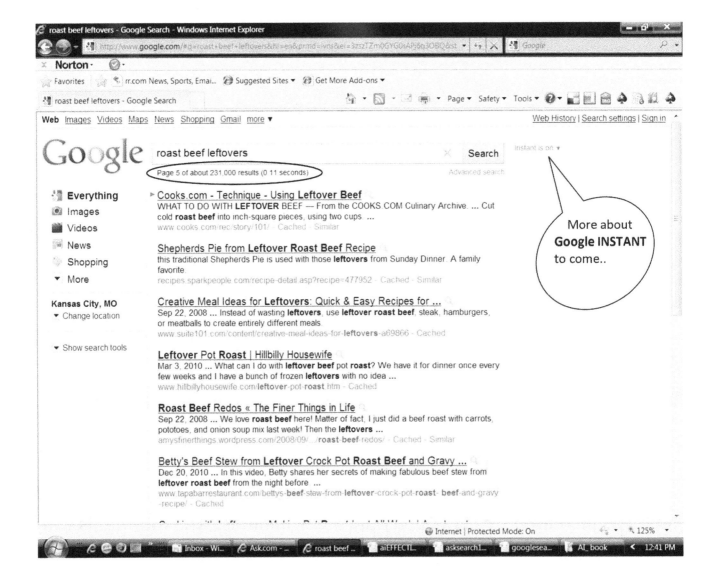

Next, we'll move on to ASK using the search words roast beef leftovers: Once more, ASK's sponsored links or ads are showcased on the top and bottom of the page.

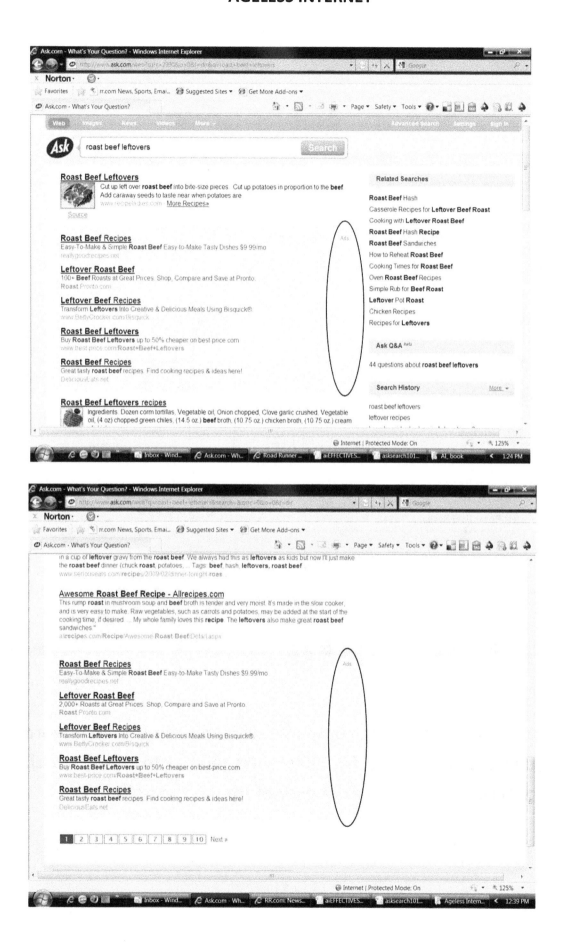

And let's look at Page 5 of the same search:

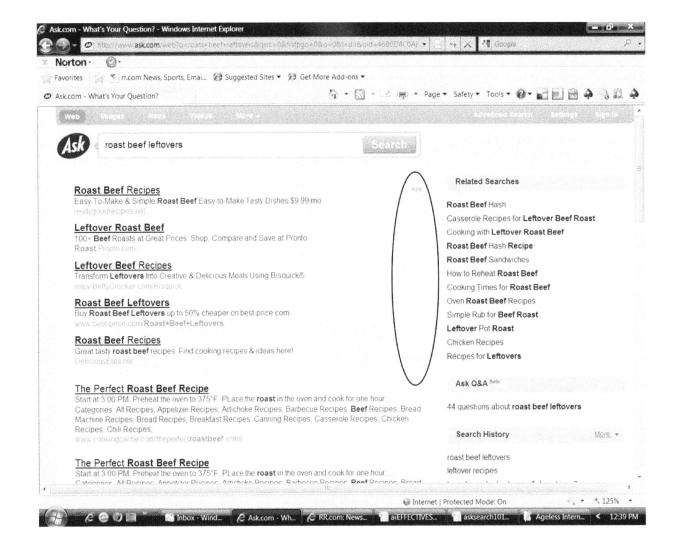

Next is a look at how Bing compares with the same search words: roast beef leftovers. Bing finds 1,350,000 results related to these search words, this search term. They show a sponsored site on the right.

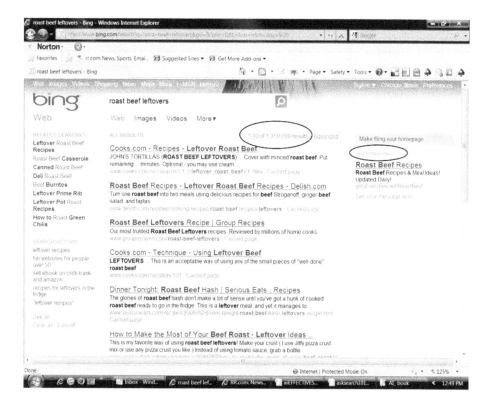

And the bottom of the first page follows here..

Following is page 5 of the search results on Bing for roast beef leftovers. Here we'll get into the meat and potatoes of searching. (Sorry, can't help myself...) ☺

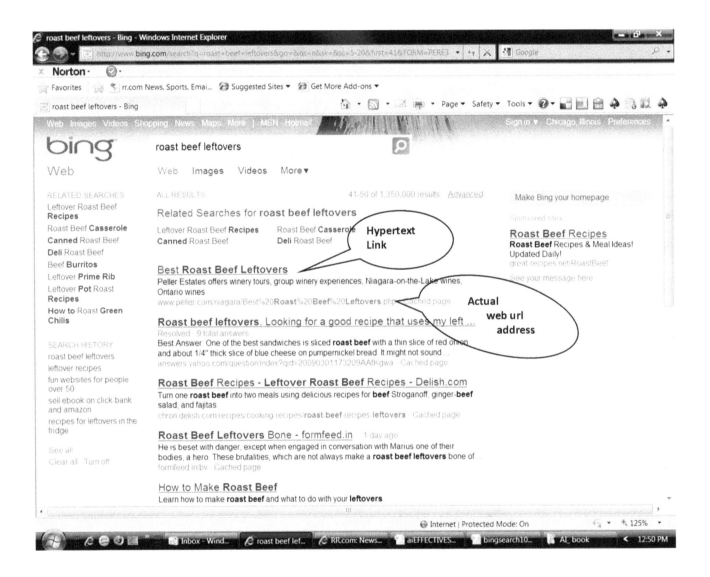

Now that you've had a chance to look at the results of three popular SEARCH ENGINES this is what I hope you've seen:

- The number of results from the search words chosen
- Bolded Blue "Hypertext Links" that will take you directly to the result (see Glossary)
- The different look from one search engine to another
- Sponsored sites

- Ads
- History of recent searches
- Related search suggestions
- How extremely fluid and changing the Internet is—really minute by minute

Using the screen shot on the previous page, from Bing's 5th page of search results for roast beef leftovers, **I want you to start looking at the ACTUAL WEB URL (ADDRESS) below the Hypertext Link.** *Do this before you click on the link.* **THIS WILL SAVE YOU A LOT OF TIME AND AGGRAVATION!**

The address at the top of the page under the bold hypertext link Best Roast Beef Leftovers reads:

www.peller.com/niagra/Best%20Roast%20Beef%20Leftovers.php

IF all you wanted to obtain was a quick, simple recipe for roast beef leftovers, this site will take you on a DETOUR. Peller is a *winery*. Now, while they are probably a fine winery, here's the point: you want a recipe for roast beef leftovers NOT an education about wine or to click on a recipe link only to be swept off to a video about a recipe! Right?

OK! Let's move on to the next web url address shown:

http://answers.yahoo.com/question/index?qid=20090301173209AAfKgwa

If you click on this link you'll wind up on Yahoo! Answers which actually *does* provide a few recipes on this site along with input you may not be interested in reading. Next is:

http://chron.delish.com/recipes/cooking-recipes/roast-beef-recipes-leftovers

And if you click on this link you're heading to the Houston Chronicle's section called Delish. Here you DO get some recipes. **The point is look before**

you click! Sometimes despite your careful observation you'll still find yourself on a site that is patently unrelated to what you want. But, by paying close attention to the address you've significantly improved your chances of successful searching!

Now, Google has a feature called "Instant"—you can see this in the screen shot on the next page. If you want this search engine to make assumptions about what you want *while you type*, choose Instant ON. If this annoys you, select OFF.   One of the cool things about it is this:

I wanted to know who wrote Wake Up Little Susie (well, I actually already knew but for those who didn't...) and before I could even finish typing what I wanted into the search bar, my answer appeared. The Everly Brothers wrote it.

I could have entered the search term: Wake Up Little Susie, who wrote? Or some such variation but right there before my eyes was the answer in Google's Instant—pretty cool, huh? Each search engine has its own features. Some you'll love, others, not so much.

Next, let's look at a search on Google for: plasma TV reviews - Results show over 3,000,000 ! Off on the right in the ADS section, you'll see www.consumerreports.org--sure they want people searching this topic to want to subscribe to their magazine or online site. They are no fools. They know that to continue to grow their brand, they need to spend ad dollars to get as much exposure as possible. As I've mentioned before, I often consult cnet and toptenreviews in addition to Consumer Reports. *It could be that they "sold" me years ago and that's why I keep coming back.* They offer good, solid data and I'm confident that they are reliable resources.

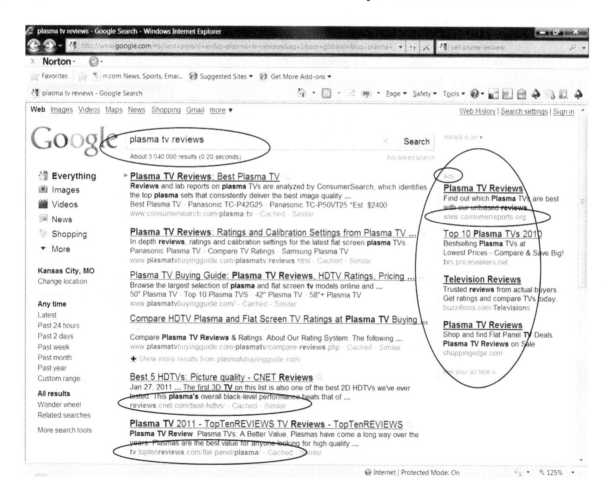

So, how many kids did Ricky & Lucy have? You could just type in Ricky & Lucy and get this:

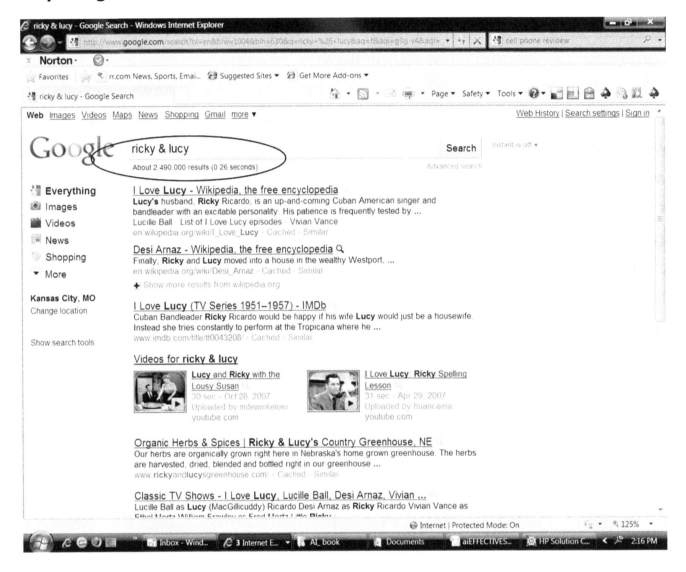

And by clicking on one link or another you will *eventually* find the answer.

Or you could type: <u>Ricky & lucy kids</u> in the search engine box and get this:

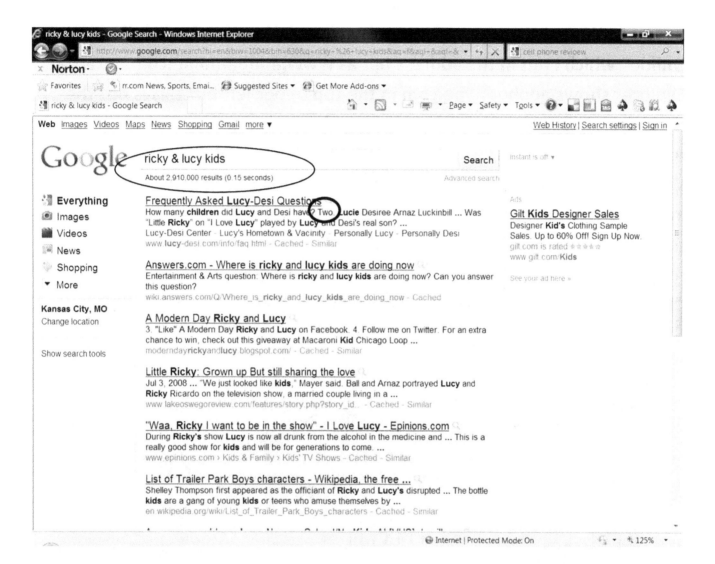

Nice, huh? Saves a little more time!

Whoa! This isn't the site I want! These days if you type in an incorrect web address you MAY get an error message letting you know you have it wrong or you MAY get MISDIRECTED. Here is an example of my looking for "Adobe Online" which I put in the address bar as www.adobeonline.com. Internet Explorer shows adobeonline.com in the top upper left but this is not the right site. _This is not the address in the address bar either._ This address reads "searchportal.information.com" which means whoever is behind this site bought the popular name knowing many people would search for this incorrectly. *My assumption* is they receive affiliate commissions whenever someone clicks on the links they offer and makes a purchase as a result.

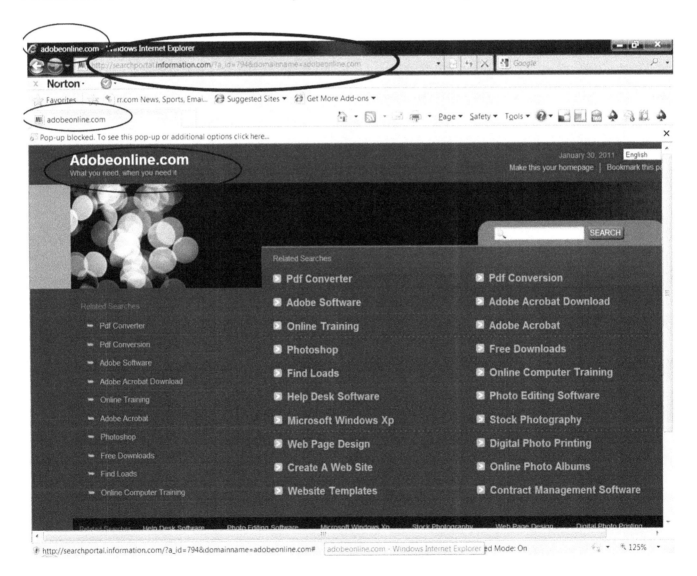

The address I really wanted is:
https://www.acrobat.com/createpdf/en/home.html and it's an awesome way to convert a variety of documents into pdfs (portable document files). This can be done for free in small amounts or you can pay monthly or annually for this terrific service. (This format is very popular because it provides nice, clean copy and because *Adobe Acrobat* **www.adobe.com** provides a free downloadable reader enabling everyone to open .pdf files.

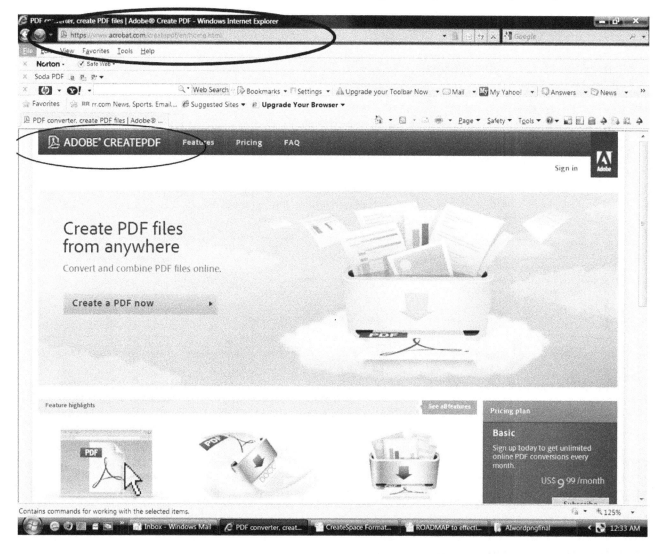

Many software programs today (like MS Word) allow you to save documents in pdf but if you don't have software, this is an alternative. Another great converting product is Soda PDF **www.sodapdf.com**. Check these out if you need to modify other file types.

Now, let's take a look at REVIEWS – for this search I'm using Metacrawler (it searches the search engines...).   I've entered the search term: *webhosting reviews.*

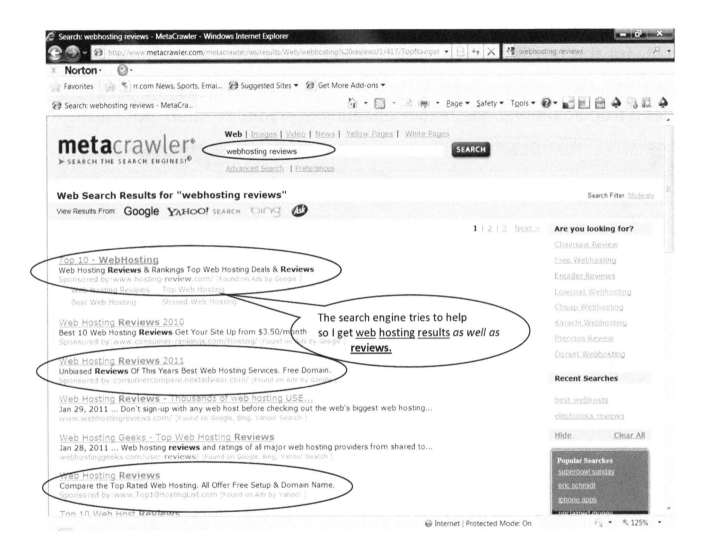

Note the addresses of these companies in the results and see where Metacrawler shows "Sponsored" which you now know means their placement in the search engines was aided by ad dollars.

There is nothing wrong with this.

Business legitimately uses advertising to promote products and services.

The point I'm making is that search engine placement doesn't indicate a better result, a more accurate result or a more worthy result.

I am 99.9% sure most of these sites will make money if you click on their link and ultimately make a purchase. This is the beauty of the Internet. There are countless ways to earn income on the Net. If done ethically, *by providing a product or service that is of value*, it's win/win for all!

A few years ago, I joined an Internet Marketing Membership Program. I paid an annual fee for the education. I learned a lot from this. I was also an affiliate for this program. To have a web presence so that I could promote it and earn affiliate income, I created a **LANDING PAGE**. This is a simple 1 or 2 page website with a message. A sales message.

Landing pages often appear in the search engine by the specific topic you want to learn about along with emotionally charged words like Scam, Fake, Revealed. Sensationalizing works in traditional print media, doesn't it? Let's say you are wondering if XYZ Internet Marketing Biz is a good investment. I'm totally making this up but if there is such a business opportunity it's purely coincidental. You may enter the search term: XYZ Internet Marketing and you could get results like: XYZ Internet Marketing Review: Scam or Is It For Real?

 Wow, you wonder, is it a scam? So you click on the link to that article & more often than not, you are assured it is NOT a scam but a real good, excellent or maybe awesome business opportunity that you should order NOW. If you click the link to BUY, this landing page did it's job, you will be whisked off to the site where you can order or maybe read the real sales letter. And the writer of that "review" will earn affiliate income for that program.

Hey, free enterprise at work, right? Right!

I only want you to know what's going on behind the scenes so you can make informed choices.

There is no right or wrong way to search – some methods produce more precise results than others. The most important things to consider when searching are:

- Use words sparingly – keep it simple
- A search engine will try to provide results for each word searched
- A search engine is not human
- While they perform the same task, search engines differ from one another
- Search engines are case insensitive (doesn't matter if you use lower or upper case)
- Search engines disregard punctuation
- Watch for sponsored sites—they can crowd out other (also) worthy sites to consider
- *Read the address (or web url) before clicking on the link to make sure it is what you are looking for!*

Happy surfing or searching…whatever you prefer to call it.

4B.

Easy Pass On The Information Superhighway

Social Media And Networking

Yes, the Internet can seem like there is a lot to learn and you may feel a little out of touch with the education system called technology. **But, keep in mind you've lived a good many years in the education system called L I F E.** This makes you perfectly suited to absorbing new information and connecting it with the stored "data" of your experience. **Don't sell yourself short!**

Remember when a new family moved to your block or development you (or your parents) would deliver some kind of goodies or gift items in a basket to welcome the newcomers to the neighborhood? This was in keeping with the tradition of the Welcome Wagon – a social visit to introduce a new family to the neighborhood and welcoming them with a basket of goods.

Most of us have attended the PTA, Girl or Boy Scouts meetings, neighborhood watch groups, Town Hall meetings, etc. Although most of these examples are focused on a cause of one kind of another, these are all social networking opportunities – *offline*.

In the 21st Century we have *online* social networking. By creating a PROFILE on a social networking site, you "put yourself on the map"—make it possible for old friends who may be looking to find you! Social networking is, in its simplest form, a communications device.

Probably the most popular social networking site today is **FACEBOOK**. A movie released in 2010 called "The Social Network" was a Golden Globe winner for best picture. It's the story of Harvard law students & Facebook co-founders Mark Zuckerberg and Eduardo Saverin and how the hugely successful site got started. The tagline "You Don't Get to 500 Million Friends Without Making a Few Enemies" is pretty pragmatic. Nominated for 8 Academy Awards, it is sure to take home some Oscar statuettes.

Why is social networking so hot?

- You can find friends from your past
- Friends from your past can find you
- You can make new friends
- You can see who is friends with whom
- You can share photos, music, videos
- You can join groups that share your interests like politics, sports, gardening
- You can engage in social networking games like FarmVille or MafiaWars

The following is a list of the TYPES of social networking sites & their web addresses for you to explore at your leisure. Most sites are free to join though they may offer activities that have fees associated with them. All will have a place for you to complete a profile about who you are and what you like. They will have a place for you to include your photo or avatar (an avatar is a computer generated or cartoon-like image representing a person, an idea, or a thing.)

Photo and other Media Sharing Sites are available for you to review without joining. If you want to upload pictures or video, you have to join. Once you join, you can interact with other members, invite friends, etc.

http://www.youtube.com YouTube Video
http://www.flickr.com   Flickr Photos

Social Bookmarking Sites permit you to save a link to the site which tells others what is of interest to you. It's like sharing your favorite recipe, article, book, picture, etc and other people can see what you've bookmarked. Bookmarking means you tag a link with key words which makes it possible for other like-minded people to find. Say you discover someone interested in restoring a 1970 Chevelle SS like you are. You can add that individual to your network so you'll be notified when they add another link.

http://www.digg.com   Digg Bookmarking Community
http://www.delicious.com   aka del.icio.us Bookmarking Community

Music Social Networking Sites are about sharing your favorite tunes with others. They act like streaming radio and attempt to gauge the music you will enjoy based on what you've shared. You create a network of people with like tastes and can share playlists with them.

http://www.pandora.com Pandora Music Network
http://www.ilike.com   iLike Music Network

And there are **Blogging Social Networking Sites** which connects individuals and their weblogs (blogs.) Instead of the standard Profile, the person keeps a running blog, writing about what interests him or her. Other users search by topic or browse blogs looking for content of interest to them. When they find something they like, that blog is added to their list— thereby becoming a friend.

http://www.blogger.com Blogger
Blogging Social Network

http://www.wordpress.com WordPress
Blogging Social Network

There are lots of social networks outside of these categories but the intent is the same. Bring together like minded individuals and give them a forum to share information and develop communities around common interests and build relationships.

Additionally, you can market your "brand" to your friends on social networking sites, for those of you with businesses or products and services to promote.

http://www.facebook.com
Facebook

http://www.myspace.com
MySpace

http://www.twitter.com
Twitter

http://www.eons.com
Eons—Social Networking for Boomers

http://www.linkedin.com LinkedIn:
business social networking

http://www.growingbolder.com
Growing Bolder

http://www.boomer-living.com
Boomer Living

http://www.egenerations.com
eGenerations

http://www.boomergirl.com
A Boomer Blogger

http://www.redwoodage.com
Redwood Age

http://www.boomerauthority.com
Boomer Authority

A 2010 study by The Pew Research Center found that social networking among people aged 50 and older had grown from 22% to an amazing 42% in the last year!

And why not? It's a perfect venue for folks whose families may be spread out across the country or even across the globe. It's ideal for connecting and reconnecting with friends, classmates, and former business associates.

Further, a digital measurement company called comScore reported 27.4 million people aged 55 and over engaged in social networking in July 2010 up from 16 million the previous year! comScore reports that 19 million people 55 and over used Facebook in July 2010 vs. 9 million the year before. *These numbers are staggering and reinforce my conviction that Ageless Internet will be of service to many Baby Boomers and Seniors.*

NOTE: With the rising popularity of Social Networking among Boomers and Seniors, and the information you are gaining here, it may become more important for you to be "turbo charged" in your Internet activity.

If you use the *most economical* (i.e. cheapest) Internet Service Provider, dial up, it may no longer serve you well. Many websites today use "flash animation" – like it sounds, it's the bells & whistles like music, graphics flashing across the screen and special lighting (like strobe) effects. If you decide to start watching online videos on your PC or Laptop, you may wish to have an ISP without restrictions to the amount of time you spend and an ISP with whom you can "fly"—not the slow poke pace of most dial up services. Blazing speed is helpful for sharing digital photos, for playing games and shopping. Internet access speed helps downloading and uploading take less time. (If you've ever visited a website where the home page appears very slowly, it's because your ISP takes longer to "load the web page.")

Again, it's your call.

Now, back to **Social Networking**. It is no secret that we are enjoying longer life spans. Today, it is not uncommon to live well into our eighties.

At this stage of our lives, and for many reasons, we may find ourselves unattached. Considering our longer life spans it makes sense that we may want to share our lives with another. Friend, lover, soul mate, husband, wife, partner, friend-with-benefits—whatever!

Internet Dating Services have made finding that other person unbelievably easy. Today, you can reach out across the country (and around the world) to meet people that share common interests with you. As with ALL exploration of the Wondrous World Wide Web, use common sense and practice safe surfing-- safe searching. Make sure you let friends and family know what you're doing. (Although this writer is happily married and has been for many years, I remember what it was like to be single.)

Don't go it alone when it comes to meeting people face to face that you "met" on the Net. Take a friend along, or meet in a very public, very neutral place. Drive yourself to the date. That way, you remain in control.

I'm no expert on this subject but I have been around the block a few times. I know that just as there are cyber thieves interested in stealing your identity online, there are con artists and thieves in the real world eager to relieve you of your bank accounts and other financial resources. **Read the security suggestions dating sites post.** You now know your way around the Net and can do your own research about safety and online dating.

I am the last person to suggest you let fear stop you from having fun! Fear is crippling, immobilizing and stops far too many of us from taking the risks necessary to enjoy the life of our dreams.

Refer to <u>Social Networking/Online Dating</u> in the SHORTCUTS TO WEBSITES OF INTEREST chapter.

Just be smart, be safe and have a great time!

4C.
Throughways: Internet Auctions & Payment
Gateway Services

Every self-respecting Boomer and Senior who has paid *any* attention to the existence of the online world in the past 16 years has heard of **eBay.**

Perhaps the most famous of Internet Auctions sites – worldwide, eBay was founded the first year my husband & I bought a home computer: 1995. By 1999, we were buying and selling on eBay. If you haven't explored this site yet, you really should! http://www.ebay.com

According to: http://auctions.nettop20.com/ eBay is the leading online auction provider in the U.S., the UK and Australia. Registered buyers and sellers on eBay have a section called "My eBay" where items they are watching, have bid on, won and need to leave feedback about, is organized.

Auction sites give users the opportunity to purchase **just about anything – from just about anywhere – for just about any amount of money.**

Registration is usually free and may be required to look around the site. (In recent years, some sites are adding monthly fees.) Sellers *normally* pay a minimum/maximum listing fee, and a min/max <u>final</u> <u>value</u> <u>fee</u>. (Meaning how much the item actually sold for.) During the auction listing process a seller may choose to add a photo, **bold** the listing headline, be included in the **"featured category"** and a few other "attention getters"– all of which come with additional fees. Some auction sites do not charge listing or selling fees, making their money through ad sponsors.

Those auctions I'm most familiar with give users the added plus of being able to leave **feedback** about the experience of the auction. Feedback motivates sellers to make accurate representation of the item up for bid, encourages good communication and swift turnaround. It takes time, courtesy, care and contact and I'm proud of our 100% feedback on eBay!

eBay Motors was added in 1999 and like its predecessor, it's hugely successful. Amazon hosts auction listings. Other popular online auction sites include:

- uBid: http://www.ubid.com
- WebStore: http://www.webstore.com
- eBid: http://www.ebid.net

- eBid US: http://us.ebid.net
- bid4assets (real estate+): http://www.bid4assets.com
- Bidz (jewelry): http://www.bidz.com
- Online Auction: http://www.onlineauction.com
- WeBidz: http://www.webidz.com
- Auctions at Overstock: http://auctions.overstock.com

At one time, Yahoo and MSN offered auction sites but they are no longer operating. There are a lot more auction sites you may want to check out. Here is a site that bills itself as the *Web Portal to the Auction Community:* http://www.internetauctionlist.com

Like everything you do on the web, use appropriate caution when giving out personal information.

I strongly suggest you use a third party payment processor (gateway service) for auction (and all your online) purchases. Always look at the address bar to make sure you are on the site intended.

Financial institutions, payment processors, etc. often show VeriSign, a lock symbol, Truste or TrustWave certified privacy, or a green highlight, etc. on the address bar or home page.

I like Paypal (having joined it before it was purchased by eBay) but there are many choices available. The beauty of a gateway service provider is that you aren't sharing your confidential credit, debit or checking account information with a large number of merchants.

By using a payment processor, your information is secure, you don't have to enter it over and over again, processing is quick and global. This type of vendor is for paying out and for receiving payments. Yes, you pay some transaction fees (depending on which side of the transaction you are on) but (in my opinion) they are quite reasonable for the simplicity and the security they provide.

As a seller, moving a lot of transactions through the service, you will probably pay a monthly fee, too.

- Paypal: https://paypal.com
- Google Checkout: https://checkout.google.com
- Intuit Go Payment: http://payments.intuit.com
- Authorize: http://www.authorize.net

Spend some time researching the services to learn what works best for you. I think you'll agree that using a Payment Gateway Service makes sense, saves time and fosters security.

4D.

Roundabouts:
A Couple Of Other Cool Things To Know About

When sending large files of photos or documents, it's best to compress (make smaller) so they don't take a long time to download or upload and they transmit quickly via email. To do this you need a **ZIP utility**—a single license program that is usually available as a free trial for 14-40 days after which you purchase and renew annually.

Manufacturers keep coming out with new & improved versions (would you expect less ?!) so upgrades are usually free throughout the year.

Zip utilities usually costs between $14.95 to $39.95 and there are some free ones, like 7-Zip below.

There are three main OS (operating systems) most of us use: Windows, Mac, and Linux. You will need a zip utility that works with your OS. I've used WinZip for years but you do have several choices :

- WinZip: http://www.winzip.com
- 7-Zip: http://www.7zip.com
- PK Zip: http://www.pkware.com/software/pkzip/

You may have heard of **Craig's List** (a classified marketplace in a community near you) where you can buy all kind of things, from home furnishings to services, find apartments, search job postings, view community events and participate in discussion forums.

Yes, there have been some tragic news stories surrounding Craig's List *but remember those are really bad people stories and sadly, happen all the time and everywhere.* Let these terrible stories serve as healthy reminders to use caution online just as we do offline.

Craig Newmark started Craig's List as a hobby in early 1995. It began as a San Francisco event listing. According to a recent check, Craig's list has over 20 billion page views per month, which translates to #7 worldwide in English language web page views per month.

The classified ads are placed by you and me (self-published) and there are 50 million U.S. users today. Craig's list is currently available in Spanish, German, Italian, French and Portuguese and per user request, has expanded its presence to 700 local sites in 70 countries. I think you'll agree, it's a place you should explore.

http://geo.craigslist.org/iso/us and *pick a city near you.* Enjoy!

4E.

Lots Of Kicks On Route 66
(Videos And Sites Of Fans)

I grew up in Illinois so it's no wonder I'm familiar with ROUTE 66. And how many of you enjoyed watching the TV program starring hunky friends George Maharis as Buz Murdock and Martin Milner as Tod Stiles? Then, later Glenn Corbett as Lincoln Case? The black & white filmed TV show ran from 1960-64 and while we never got to look too deep into the characters, they represented restless youth looking for meaning in life.   Imagine that..   ;-)

When Pixar's movie Cars came out, interest in the historic highway was re-kindled and it introduced new generations to Route 66! I hope these links to YouTube videos and focused websites are of interest.

http://www.youtube.com/watch?v=R_ykDw-06H8
A TV intro

http://www.youtube.com/watch?v=dCYApJtsyd0
Nat King Cole singing Route 66

http://www.youtube.com/watch?v=kLUYf6cekMA   &feature=related:
Bobby Troupe singing Route 66

http://www.youtube.com/watch?v=tg2EbJy-9dc&feature=related:
Chuck Berry singing Route 66

And here are the _true fans and experts_ of the famous ROUTE 66:

http://www.national66.com/index.html
The National Historic Route 66 Federation

http://www.historic66.com/
The Mother Road

http://www.legendsofamerica.com/66-main.html
Travelling the Mother Road

http://rwarn17588.wordpress.com/schedule-of-route-66-events/
An Oklahoman and his wife preserving Route 66 – bravo!

CHAPTER FIVE: GLOSSARY

5A.

Glossary

Lingo You May Want To Know

🛡 APPLICATION is a software program or group of programs intended for end users. Often broken down into two classes as either (operating) systems software or application software. Word processing programs, graphics, spreadsheets and games are all applications.

🛡 BOTS are part of a network of infected machines called "Botnets." While similar to Trojans and worms, they sneak onto unprotected computers by email from an already infected computer, downloaded by a Trojan or installed by a malevolent website.

🛡 BYTES refer to a unit of storage known as binary term- able to hold a single character.   Large amounts of memory are indicated by kilobytes (1,024 bytes,) megabytes (1,048,576 bytes,) and gigabytes (1,073,741,824 bytes.)

BROWSER is a type of software that helps you see, hear, find, record material on the World Wide Web. Popular browsers include Microsoft Internet Explorer, Mozilla Firefox, Apple Safari and others.

CD stands for compact disc. You may see CD-ROM (Read Only Memory) and CD-R (Recordable) CD-RW (Re-writable.) You may see them with + or with − signs before the R or RW.   (For more detailed information about compact discs, you might want to check out Andy McFadden's www.cdrfaq.org)

CHAT ROOM is a method of communicating with other users in "real time" vs. delayed time, as with email. Chat rooms exist for a huge variety of topics and admission is generally open to anyone. Your comment appears to everyone in the chat room so you don't know who will read or respond to the messages. Caution is in order here.

CYBERCRIME is online fraud. Cybercriminals use bots, Trojan horses and spyware to attack.

CYBERSPACE refers to the electronic areas, communities and the culture on computer networks, like the Internet.

DNS means Domain Name Server, introduced in 1984 to permit individual domain names.

DVD stands for digital versatile disc.

EMAIL stand for electronic mail sent from one computer user to another. Email may contain word based messages, attachments like photographs, or reports and other forms of multimedia. You must have a *modem* from an *Internet Service Provider*.

🛣️ FAQ stands for Frequently Asked Questions. Many websites have an FAQ page – often invaluable. Depending on the site, many common questions are addressed on these pages, streamlining the information process.

🛣️ FORUM (WEB) a meeting place or community online for sharing point of view

🛣️ HARDWARE refers to the nuts and bolts of equipment, the computer processor, monitor and other peripherals like scanners and printers.

🛣️ HOME PAGE while often used as the default page for the browser you are using, it is also the introductory or first page of a website owned by a business, individual or organization.

🛣️ HTML means *hypertext mark-up language*. This is a document format for the World Wide Web. Text must be converted to HTML to be readable on the web.

🛣️ HYPERLINK is one or more words, highlighted and underlined in text on the screen. Clicking on a hyperlink takes you directly to another source of information. Sometimes, this hyperlink opens in a new window; sometimes you are taken from the webpage you were on to the linked one.

🛣️ INFORMATION SUPERHIGHWAY a term coined by Al Gore to represent a global, high speed network of computers serving millions of users simultaneously, transmitting email, voice, video and other multimedia. This system links schools, hospitals, business and government around the world. The U.S. Government's official term for this is "National Information Infrastructure" or NII.

🛣️ INTERNET the largest computer network in the world.

INTERNET SERVICE PROVIDER (ISP) is a generic term for a provider connecting a user to the Internet, usually for a fee. Recognizable ISPs include America Online (AOL) Yahoo, and Earthlink to name a few.

MALWARE a category of malicious code that includes worms, viruses, and Trojan Horses seeks to remain undetected on your system

MODEM is a device that permits computers to communicate with other computers over telephone or cable lines and other delivery systems. Modems come in different speeds: the higher the speed, the faster the connection. "Dial-up" uses telephone lines and it typically the slowest connection speed.

MOUSE is the small device connected by a cord to your computer allowing you to give commands to the computer. There are many different kinds available.

MULTIMEDIA refers to a combination of two or more information types like text and images, video and audio.

NET is shortened version of Internet

NETIQUETTE stands for good manners on the Internet or in cyberspace. Netiquette is "enforced" by other users.

OFFLINE means working on your computer doing things like word-processing while you are not connected to the Internet.

ONLINE any and all activities performed while connected to the Internet.

OS is Operating System (Example: Microsoft's Windows or Apple's Macintosh or Mac)

🛣 PASSWORD a confidential word or series of alpha numeric characters that permits access to sites. This is usually used in conjunction with your email address or a User ID.

🛣 PC stands for personal computer. Initially combined with IBM as in IBM PC or IBM compatible personal computers or Intel-compatible personal computers. This excludes other types of personal computers like Mac.

🛣 PHISHING is an online con game by technologically knowledgeable con artists and identity thieves. It can be in the form of an instant message, spam, email or hateful website and *tricks people into revealing sensitive information like credit card numbers* or *banking information*. Phishing attempts often come with a warning that prompts the user to respond, such as your membership will be revoked, or your account suspended. In the body of the phishing email will be a hyperlink. The link will transport you to *what appears to be the legitimate site*. You'll be instructed to provide personal info like a Social Security, credit card or bank account numbers, etc. NOTE: established, legitimate firms will <u>not</u> contact you in this manner.

🛣 PORTAL (WEB) often called a gateway or entrance to the World Wide Web or some other large online community

🛣 POST adding information to a forum, your blog, etc.

🛣 SEARCH ENGINE is a program that performs Internet searches based on criteria the user provides. Example Google is a search engine.

🛣 SERVER is a host computer that stores information and software programs that may be accessed by users of other computers.

🛣 SOFTWARE refers to instructions for use on your hardware. There are many types of software. Application software is used to do word processing (MS Word) or to play games while Operating System software is required to run the computer itself. (Windows or MAC) Today, software can be preinstalled on a computer, downloaded or may be on a CD.

SPAM is unwanted email sent to our inbox (often without an address in the To or Cc fields and sent to a large number of recipients) which should be deleted immediately. It is a security concern and a vehicle for sending malware, spyware, and focused phishing attempts.

SPYWARE seeks to remain undetected and can be downloaded from instant messaging, email messages, file sharing connections and even when accepting End User License Agreements from software programs.

TROJAN HORSE is malware that is usually dropped from websites

URL stands for Uniform Resources Locator. This is an address of a site on the Internet. Example: http://www.agelessinternet.com

USERID or USER ID the name you choose to log on with. Many sites require you to pick a User ID before proceeding to download or access information from them.

This is especially true of sites where you can make purchases or those to which you pay a fee to belong. (Example: eBay Auctions or ConsumerReports.Org)

VIRTUAL (as in "virtual reality") an artificial environment created with software that provides the user with an experience that persuades him he is truly experiencing reality—a simulated environment created for educational purposes or an imagined one for a game or interactive story.

VIRUS malware that infects downloaded files

WEB short for World Wide Web

WEB SITES are locations on the World Wide Web that may provide basic information or be very *interactive* with graphics, sounds, shopping carts, and links to other sites. The address will begin with three "w's" www.agelessinternet.com or may appear as a complete URL (see above)

WORM is malware that is often sent through email and instant messages

WWW stands for World Wide Web, an HTML based navigation system that must conform to universal standards, permitting most browsers access to a variety of linked resources on the Internet.

CHAPTER SIX:
SHORTCUTS

6A.
Shortcuts To Websites Of Interest

This chapter is intended as a resource for you. While I'm familiar with many of these 150+ sites, I can't tell you I've visited all of them. This is for informational purposes and to help you get used to exploring the Internet quickly. Type these addresses into the address bar of your computer's browser, then click the arrow or hit enter and you'll be on the site.)

The *most common* web addresses in the world will end with the extension "**.com.**" There is also

- .org
- .net
- .info
- .biz
- .us
- .int

.mobi

.me

.edu

and .gov – most specifically in the U.S.

NEW EXTENSIONS ARE ADDED REGULARLY..

Most non-profits will use **.org** for organization, but some businesses do, too. Educational institutions will have **.edu** extensions while the US Government's Websites will end in **.gov**.

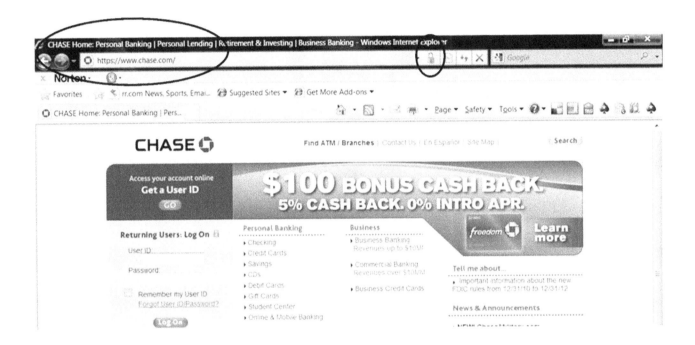

Different countries often have a 2 character designation in addition to the main address to designate their country, as in .ca for Canada.

ALWAYS look at the domain name in the address bar to make sure you are on the website you intend to be on. (Simple misspellings can take you to an entirely different website- see phishing in the chapter called ROAD BLOCKS- cleverly designed to appear exactly like your financial institution or other "trusted" site... Then, when you submit your user ID and password, the thieves obtain secure information they can use for Identity Theft.)

SO, WHENEVER YOU ARE PERFORMING A SEARCH, LOOK AT THE AD-DRESS OF THE RESULTS BEFORE CLICKING ON THE LINK. IF GOING TO A SE-CURE SITE LIKE YOUR BANK, MAKE SURE THE CORRECT INSTITUTION AP-PEARS IN THE ADDRESS BAR AT THE TOP & YOU SEE A SECURE SYMBOL, LIKE A LOCK.

FOR THAT MATTER ALWAYS LOOK AT THE ADDRESS BAR TO BE SURE YOU ARE WHERE YOU WANT TO BE ALL THE TIME. *Occasionally there will be a different name but it should closely resemble what you were after.*

There is a separate chapter to help you get the most out of the search process elsewhere in this book.

Following are loads of websites that may be of interest to you.

I've attempted to list a variety of sites of interest to Baby Boomers and Seniors. Writing this chapter could have taken forever – there are so many sites in cyber space. Think of it like a cafeteria where you look at the variety of foods available. You will not like everything you see, so pick & choose only what you want. This list scarcely scratches the surface of what is available on the Net. **It's like a pinhole view.**

I hope you find some of this useful, informational and downright **F U N !**

AGING (consider the alternative! ☺)

http://www.age-well.org/
Age-Well, Stay Younger Longer, Keep Active and Healthy a non-profit site

http://www.suddenlysenior.com
"The daily ezine for everyone over 50 who feels way too young to be old."

http://www.aarp.org
American Association of Retired Persons

http://games.aarp.org
Brain teasers to keep our minds sharp

http://www.happy-neuron.com
Brain fitness exercises for all ages (free membership) plus online store

http://www.50plus.com
"Everything You Need to Know"

http://www.seniorcorps.gov
National & Community Service

http://www.over50web.net
"50 Plus, Loud and Proud"

http://www.seniorjournal.com
"Senior Citizen News and Information Daily on the Web"

http://www.seniormag.com
Senior Magazine Online

http://www.todaysenior.com
A Wordpress site with topics of interest to Boomers and Seniors

http://www.life-over-50.com
A Senior Chat Room

http://www.boomerauthority.com
Boomer Authority – "Providing Boomers with Timely Advice When They Need It Most"

ALSO see Social Networking

ANCESTRY: Finding Our Roots

http://www.ancestry.com
Largest family-history resource online - available by subscription ($13/month as of this writing)

http://www.archives.gov/genealogy
US Government site helping family historians by providing National Archive records

http://www.Facebook.com
application called FamilyLink

CAREGIVING

http://www.silvercensus.com
Silver Census – The Premier Resource for Senior Living and Health Services

http://www.aplaceformom.com
A Place for Mom, Dad, or anyone you want to help

http://www.caregiver.org
Family Caregiver Alliance

http://www.eldercare.gov
US Government resource for community services

http://www.eldercarelink.com
Portal to services for boomers and seniors

http://www.caremanager.org
Professional Geriatric Care Managers Assoc

http://www.seniorcorp.com
"Changing the Way America Ages"

COMPUTING

http://www.eff.org
Looking out for our digital rights

http://www.ageinplacetech.com
Aging In Place Technology Watch

http://www.microsoft.com
Microsoft Corp

http://www.apple.com
Apple Computers et al

http://www.professorteaches.com
Professor Teaches CD education on all major software programs

DICTIONARY

http://www.netdictionary.com/
by Albion.com and Seth T. Ross

http://www.merriam-webster.com
Merriam-Webster Dictionary and Thesaurus

http://dictionary.cambridge.org/
Cambridge Dictionary & Thesaurus Online

http://oxforddictionaries.com/
Oxford Dictionary Online

DRIVING DIRECTIONS & MAPS

http://www.mapquest.com
Mapquest

http://www.maps.google.com
Google Maps

http://www.maps.com
Maps

E-CARDS/ECARDS (Electronic cards)

http://www.jacquielawson.com
Totally Unique Animated Cards -my personal favorite- annual subscription

http://www.smilebox.com
Pay as you go, subscription, some free options, add your own pictures
to cards

http://www.123greetings.com/
"Free Greetings for the Planet"

http://www.care2.com/ecards
Great green organization, care2

http://www.bluemountain.com
This is the company that changed cards forever in the 70s-growing into the
21st century)

http://www.angelwinks.net
Heavenly Post Card Shoppe. There are many, many options in ecards or
epostcards. Every large, self-respecting greeting card manufacturer has added ecards to their product offering.

EDUCATION

http://www.nces.ed.gov
National Center for Education Statistics

http://www.ed.gov
Department of Education

http://www.thefreedictionary.com/education
Free Dictionary

http://en.wikipedia.org/wiki/Wikipedia:About
Before reading & relying on information from this source, read
"About Wikipedia"

http://www.wikipedia.org
Free Content Encyclopedia openly written edited by you & me

http://www.sylvanlearning.com
Learning assistance for children at every grade

http://www.about.com
Info portal written by people with expertise in specific areas and follow
an ethics model

http://www.acenet.edu
American Council on Education

http://www.webopedia.com
Web Encyclopedia

FINANCE & INVESTING

http://www.worldbank.org/
World Bank

http://www.kiplinger.com
Kiplinger newsletter

http://online.wsj.com/home-page/
Wall Street Journal

http://money.cnn.com/
Money

http://www.forbes.com
Forbes

http://www.fool.com
Motley Fool

FUN, ENTERTAINING (and A LITTLE wacky too)

http://www.despair.com
Demotivators Products

http://www.2leep.com
A blog hub of stories from around the world

http://www.nascar.com
Nascar Online

http://www.cheezeburger.com/sites
Wild & wacky: 50 websites like TherelFixedlt (redneck repairs) and
TotallyLooksLike

http://www.allrecipes.com
Just what it sounds like ☺

http://www.popcapgames.com
Free (& cash) games site – play online or download- featuring totally
absorbing "Bejeweled"

http://www.historychannel.com
As I've gotten older, history is pretty darn interesting! You?

http://www.fark.com
Website of the slogan "It's not news, it's Fark"

http://www.wonderhowto.com
A community energized search engine & directory for free how to information & video

http://www.youtube.com
Every possible type of video you can image from hilarious to disastrous

http://www.nationalgeographic.com
National Geographic – a world of information

http://www.bored.com
100% free fun games

GAS GAUGE WATCHERS

http://www.gasbuddy.com
Gas Buddy

http://www.cost2drive.com
Cost 2 Drive

http://www.tripadvisor.com/tankofgas
Trip Advisor's Tank of Gas

GOVERNMENT SITES U.S.

http://www.whitehouse.gove
Official website of the U.S. White House

http://www.senate.gov
Official website of the U.S. Senate

http://www.house.gov
Official website of the U.S. House of Representatives

http://www.medicare.gov/
Government site for medicare

http://my.medicare.gov/
Official site for individual Medicare recipients

http://www.cms.hhs.gov/
Centers for Medicare and Medicaid Health & Human Services

http://www.medicare.gov/pdphome.asp
Prescription drug plan

http://www.nasa.gov
National Aeronautics and Space Administration

http://www.ssa.gov
Social Security

http://www.healthfinder.gov
Health & Human Services Department

http://www.cdc.gov/
Center for Disease Control

http://www.nih.gov
National Institute of Health

http://www.health.gov/
US Government Health

http://www.nimh.nih.gov/
National Institute of Mental Health

http://www.nlm.nih.gov/
National Library of Medicine

http://www.medlineplus.gov/
from National Institute & National Library of Health

HEALTH & MEDICAL RELATED SITES

http://www.medicarerights.org/
Non-profit dedicated to ensuring your rights

http://www.medicareadvocacy.org/
Established in 1986, organization for Senior advocacy

http://www.medicare.org/
Consumer beneficiary site

http://www.webmd.com/
online portal for accessing health related information- no substitute for doctor

http://www.mayoclinic.com/
Mayo Clinic

http://www.who.int
World Health Organization

http://www.hopkinsmedicine.org
John Hopkins medicine

http://www.silvercensus.com
Premier Resource for Senior Living and Health Services

JOB- RELATED

http://www.workgoesstrong.com
Work (Home, Family, Healthy, Style, Life, Tech and Play) Goes Strong

http://www.workforce50.com
Work Force for 50+

http://www.jobsover50.com
"The Source for Hiring Baby Boomers and Retirees"

http://www.retirementjobs.com
"Jobs for People Over 50"

http://www.retireeworkforce.com
Job Database

http://www.boomercareer.com
Primarily Articles & Resources

http://www.wiserworker.com
"Live Young, Work Wiser"

http://www.seniors4hire.org
"Online community for those 50 and older & the companies that want to recruit them."

MUSEUMS

http://www.louvre.fr
(select English to visit the Louvre's website)

http://www.si.edu
Smithsonian Institution

http://www.mfa.org
Museum of Fine Arts – Boston

http://www.amnh.org
American Museum of Natural History- NY

http://www.msichicago.org
Museum of Science & Industry Chicago

http://www.museumoflight.org
Museum of Flight

http://www.getty.edu/museum
The J. Paul Getty Museum

NETIQUETTE (Networking Etiquette)

http://tools.ietf.org/html/rfc1855
(original document encouraging respectful communication across the Net by (then) Intel employee, Sally Hambridge)

http://www.albion.com/netiquette/
Core Netiquette "Rules"

http://www.netmanners.com/
Net Manners

PETS and ANIMALS

http://cuteoverload.com/
Too funny pictures of animals

http://www.acfacat.com/
American Cat Fanciers Association

http://www.cfa.org
Cat Fanciers Association

http://www.akc.org
American Kennel Club

http://akccar.org
Companion Animal Recovery

http://www.akc.org/meet_the-breeds/
Meet the Breeds event sponsored by AKC & CFA

http://www.petsmd.com
Information about pet health-no substitution for Vet

http://www.pethealth.org
More information about pet health-no substitution for Vet

http://www.petloss.com
Coping with the loss of your pet

http://www.rainbowbridge.org
The original Rainbow Bridge pet memorial site

http://www.rainbowsbridge.com
Another person's take on a pet memorial site

NOTE: There are many wonderful (and sadly, many wasteful) organizations whose focus is on **animal welfare**. I'm a huge advocate of ANIMAL WELFARE but also of giving wisely. After a quarter century supporting one of the biggest names in this category, I withdrew my support. I want to see at least

75% of all donations going to the cause. More overhead than that is unacceptable by way of membership mismanagement (getting 2 & 3 mailings in a short time span asking me to join after being a member over 20 years) or huge salaries and bonuses for administrators. If you agree start checking http://www.charitywatch.org before you choose to support a cause. They don't cover all charitable organizations but they cover a lot.

REFERENCE SITES

http://www.pewinternet.org/
Pew Research Center & American Life Project

http://www.rand.org/
Rand Corporation

http://www.bbb/org/us
Better Business Bureau

http://www.consumerreports.org/
Subscription based unbiased product and service reviews

http://reviews.cnet.com/
product review site with pricing (a property of CBS Interactive)

http://www.pcmag.com
Personal Computing Digital Magazine

http://www.charitywatch.org
See how your favorite charity performs – give wisely!

SOCIAL NETWORKING/ONLINE DATING

http://www.eons.com
Online Community for Baby Boomers

http://www.facebook.com
Facebook

http://www.boomerauthority.com
Boomer Authority

http://www.seniorfriendfinder.com
Personal Ads site

http://www.fun-over-50.com
the US version of this international dating portal

http://www.wiredseniors.com
"A web of your own"

http://www.boomercupid.com
"Safe network for meeting 40+ mature singles"

http://www.overfifties.com
"Your worldwide connection."

http://www.seniorpeoplemeet.com
"The #1 dating community for seniors."

http://www.babyboomer-dating.com
"Just for baby boomers – for dating, travel and activity partners"

http://www.seniormatch.com
"Safe Network for Meeting 50+ Young and Passionate Singles!"

http://www.seniordatelink.com
"Where sexy singles meet"

ONLINE DATING FOR GENERAL POPULATION
(including Boomers & Seniors)

http://www.match.com
Match

http://www.zoosk.com
Zoosk

http://www.eharmony.com eHarmony

ALSO see AGING

TRAVEL

http://www.travel.com
Travel Online

http://www.orbitz.com
Orbitz

http://www.priceline.com
Priceline (Discount Travel)

http://www.tripadvisor.com
Trip Advisor News & Reviews

http://www.transitionsabroad.com/listings/travel/senior/index.shtml
"Work, Study, Travel, Living"

http://www.randmcnally.com
Travel Planning and Maps

http://www.roadsideamerica.com/ "Your online guide to offbeat tourist attractions."

WEATHER

http://www.weather.com
National Weather Channel

http://www.weather.gov
National Oceanic & Atmospheric Administration's Weather

http://www.weather.org
"Weather Forecast and Climate History"

http://www.wunderground.com
Weather Underground

http://www.intellicast.com
"The Authority in Expert Weather"

Your feedback is welcome. Let me know if any of these links are invalid by writing: correct@agelessinternet.com.

THANK YOU for reading **Ageless Internet**. By now, you should feel well equipped to navigate the Net on your own. I've shown you:

- which **Internet Security** programs will keep you safe
- **terminology** that will ease you into the 21st century
- **how to effectively perform an Internet search**
- how to **maximize the time you invest "online"**
- how to locate **authentic review sites** and affiliate review sites
- What ISP (Internet Service Provider) options you have and their differences

- provided **over 150 interesting and informative website** options
- introduced you to **social networking, auctions, payment gateways** & MORE

I hope you've found this information useful and of value to you. *Your feed-back is welcome.* Please drop a line at: comments@agelessinternet.com

~To Your Safe & Exhilarating Internet Journey~

-Terry Lynne Hale

CHAPTER SEVEN: JOURNEY'S END

And the beginning of YOUR Internet exploration..

"Well if you ever plan to motor west
Just take my way that's the highway that's the best
<u>Get your kicks on Route 66</u>
Well it winds from Chicago to L.A.
More than 2000 miles all the way
<u>Get your kicks on Route 66</u>
Well goes from St. Louie down to Missouri
Oklahoma city looks oh so pretty
You'll see Amarillo and Gallup, New Mexico
Flagstaff, Arizona don't forget Winona
<u>Kingman, Barstow, San Bernadino</u>
Would you get hip to this kindly tip
And go take that California trip

Get your kicks on Route 66

Well goes from St. Louie down to Missouri

Oklahoma city looks oh so pretty

You'll see Amarillo and Gallup, New Mexico

Flagstaff, Arizona don't forget Winona

Kingman, Barstow, San Bernadino

Would you get hip to this kindly tip

And go take that California trip

Get your kicks on Route 66"

-by Bobby Troup (published 1946)

ABOUT THE AUTHOR

Terry Lynne Hale has over 30 years of sales, marketing, writing, research and training experience in a variety of industries. She thrives on sharing information and credits many authors with being instrumental in developing the person she is today. Passions include family, the Internet, pets, the Internet, the planet, the Internet, writing, the Internet, publishing, the Internet, marketing, the Internet, Boomer and Senior health and living issues, and the Internet. Her never-ending quest for learning led her to explore the WWW after buying her first computer in 1995. Naturally, she wanted to share her enthusiasm for the Internet with others. Her freelance writing and desktop publishing business can be found at www.care2shareNOW.com. Additionally, Hale is a Diamond Ezine Articles author and is the Boomer Care Advisor for Silver Census. She has published 4 Squidoo lenses to date. Her training and writing background fueled the passion that led her to write and publish her first book:

Ageless Internet: *Internet BASICS for Boomers and Seniors.*

NOTES

NOTES

TERRY LYNNE HALE

NOTES

www.ingramcontent.com/pod-product-compliance
Lightning Source LLC
Chambersburg PA
CBHW080425060326
40689CB00019B/4388